Joseph G. Carrigan

Cheat Mountain

Or, Unwritten Chapter of the Late War

Joseph G. Carrigan

Cheat Mountain
Or, Unwritten Chapter of the Late War

ISBN/EAN: 9783743394834

Manufactured in Europe, USA, Canada, Australia, Japa

Cover: Foto ©ninafisch / pixelio.de

Manufactured and distributed by brebook publishing software (www.brebook.com)

Joseph G. Carrigan

Cheat Mountain

CHEAT MOUNTAIN;

OR,

UNWRITTEN CHAPTER OF THE LATE WAR.

BY A MEMBER OF THE BAR,

FAYETTEVILLE, TENN.

NASHVILLE:
ALBERT B. TAVEL, STATIONER AND PRINTER.
1885.

PART I.
CHEAT MOUNTAIN.

CHEAT MOUNTAIN.

PERHAPS no greater injustice has been done to any portion of the Confederate troops than to the officers and men composing the Eighth and Sixteenth Regiments of Tennessee Infantry, by writers of Confederate history, in failing to recite their memorable campaign in the mountains of Northwestern Virginia, in the fall and winter of 1861.

The long silence of history, whatever may have been the cause, has induced the writer to make an effort to rescue from oblivion the heroic deeds and sufferings of those noble men.

It may be true, however, that the real and true facts connected with this particular campaign or service have never been told, and hence the whole chapter, to call it such, is about to pass away unnoticed and unwritten.

Over twenty-four years have now passed away since these two regiments made one of the most wonderful and daring campaigns over those mountains ever made by any troops in this or any other country. The soldiers who engaged or participated in these marches and great hardships are rapidly passing away, falling one by one, until but few remain to bear testimony to the sufferings endured by them and their comrades during their eventful struggles on Cheat Mountain.

Nothing like a perfect or exact history can now be given, for many of the incidents have passed from memory, and upon this, to a great extent, we are compelled to rely. Having gathered up fragments here and there, and while very unsatisfactory to us, we shall strive to do whatever we can, in detailing this campaign in the mountains. We desire here to say, in attempting this brief and necessarily imperfect history of this march, we hope we will be pardoned for awarding to the humble soldier in the ranks his due share of honor, for in war as almost everything else, he is made the hewer of wood and drawer of water, and his merits are too often overlooked and undue prominence given to his superiors in command.

In this march, it is due for us to say, however, that almost all men were on a level, and when fairly out into the vast chain of mountains and wild woods, and in deep, dismal hollows, every man was his own captain, and with only one command: "Boys, keep your eyes on your guns!"

Before proceeding further, we take the liberty to say, that what was designated in the Confederate army as Donelson's Brigade, was composed of the Eighth and Sixteenth Regiments of Tennessee Volunteers, commanded by Cols. Alf. S. Fulton and John H. Savage. Col. Boneley's regiment, from Georgia, did not remain with us long, and did not participate in the marches and hardships we shall attempt to narrate, because of unusual sickness and deaths.

The Eighth Tennessee Regiment was composed of the following companies from Lincoln county, and the other companies will be noticed in their proper places. We give as complete lists of the officers and men as we are able to get from authentic sources:

HALL'S COMPANY (B.)

OFFICERS.

A. M. HALL, Captain.
CHRIS. C. MCKINNEY, First Lieutenant.
T. W. BLEDSOE, Second Lieutenant.
C. N. ALLEN, Third Lieutenant.
N. P. KOONCE, Orderly Sergeant.
T. F. HARRIS, Second Sergeant.
C. M. BUCHANAN, Third Sergeant.
S. J. LEONARD, Fourth Sergeant.
C. B. METCALFE, First Corporal.
W. T. WOODRUFF, Second Corporal.
D. T. EASTLAND, Third Corporal.
C. W. GILL, Fourth Corporal.

PRIVATES.

Allen, Richard.
Bates, N. B.
Blake, W. C.
Blakemore, H. A.
Branson, A. J.
Boyle, Patrick.
Buchanan, J. D.
Brewer, J. F.
Brewer, Green.
Bradford, John.
Blackwell, T. O.
Blackshear, Elisha.
Bonner, A. J.
Brown, J. W.
Cummings, J. J.

Keeler, J. B.
Locker, R. A.
Locker, W. L.
Morrison, W. B.
McEwen, J. G.
McEwen, E. C.
Mitchell, Jesse.
Merrit, W. H.
McCants, W. P.
Mathews, R. M.
Malear, B. E.
Moore, J. A.
Morton, J. A.
Morton, James.
Maulding, J. H.

Craig, Wm.
Carmack, G. C.
Capps, M. V. B.
Cumberland, Jas.
Elliot, J. F.
Fulton, A. S., (Col.)
Freeman, W. J.
Greer, Jno. T.
Greer, John R.
Glidewell, F. W.
Gilbert, W. A.
Gibson, J. F.
Hanaway, T. H. C.
Hanaway, E. H. W.
Hester, T. G.
Hardin, J. R.
Hall, J. M.
Isom, W. P.
Jones, J. M.
Jeeter, J. T.

Nichols, John.
Nichols, W. H.
Pigg, Claiborne.
Porter, G. W.
Pitcock, W. P.
Quarles, W. F.
Quarles, R. A.
Rives, J. M.
Rives, R. C.
Robinson, J. F.
Roach, B. T.
Reynolds, S. R.
Scott, J. W.
Scott, N. B.
Scott, Alex.
Sanders, Wm.
Watson, W. F.
Watson, J. B.
Wells, Harrison.

McKINNEY'S COMPANY (C.)

OFFICERS.

RANE McKINNEY, Captain.
N. M. BEARDEN, First Lieutenant.
T. W. RANEY, Second Lieutenant.
A. M. DOWNING, Third Lieutenant.
R. D. HARDIN, Orderly Sergeant.
W. J. KING, Second Sergeant.
L. J. E. BEARDEN, Third Sergeant.
J. W. RAWLS, Fourth Sergeant.
W. C. BRIGHT, First Corporal.
J. H. FLETCHER, Second Corporal.
D. C. DEWITT, Third Corporal.
J. M. SHORT, Fourth Corporal.

PRIVATES.

Beech, A. C.
Billions, J.
Bland, W. J.
Blankenship, Jno.
Blankenship, T. F.
Blair, W. B.
Branson, J. K.
Bryan, J. H. C.
Brown, J. S.
Burns, J. H.
Byers, J. M.
Carpenter, E. M.
Caughran, J. F.
Coats, J. B.
Colbert, J. C.
Coley, W. H.
Commons, A. J.
Coulahan, F. G.
Dollar, J. P.
Daniel, Robt.
Dosier, C. M.
Downing, F. M.
Doyle, Mike.
Dunn, G. W.
Flannigan, Peter.
Flemming, J. W.
Flynt, Navins.
George, J. H.
George, W. B.
Gee, Thos.
Gray, H. H.
Gray, J. H.
Gray, J. P.
Griffis, T. P.
Grubbs, W. J.
Howell, Sam.
Howell, Sol.
Jamison, J. W.
Jones, E. F.
Kelly, John.
Kennedy, Michael.
Key, C. G.
Key, Manly.
Locker, J. H.
Maddox, J. J.
Maddox, N. G.
Marberry, Len.
Marlow, J. A.
Maroney, J. C.
McAnn, S. F.
McAlister, Sam.
McDaniel, Henry.
McDaniel, J. Y.
McFerran, J. M.
Moore, Joe.
Neeves, R. C.
Phillips, E. J.
Pucket, A. H.
Raney, W. J.
Sandlin, J. T.
Saterfield, Jno.
Shay, Syl.
Simmons, Wm.
Smith, Stephen.
Spray, Lewis.
Steadman, N. P.
Stewart, W. L.
Sullivan, Thos.
Thomas, W. C.
Thornton, F. M.

Gulley, J. J.
Hamilton, W. H.
Halbert, J. T.
Hall, J. A.
Harbison, D. C.
Henderson, J. W.
Hovis, J. R.
Howell, B. T.

Toon, J. P.
Vickers, W. T.
Wallace, J. P.
Walker, A. L.
Warren, Thos.
Watson, Wm.
Wrigart, J. M.
Womack, H. W.

HIGGINS' COMPANY (G.)

OFFICERS.

Geo. W. Higgins, Captain.
W. C. Griswell, First Lieutenant.
David Sullivan, Second Lieutenant.
E. S. N. Bobo, Brevet Second Lieutenant.
Jo. G. Carrigan, Orderly Sergeant.
M. C. Shook, Second Sergeant.
T. L. Williamson, Third Sergeant.
Francis Wells, Fourth Sergeant.
M. C. Cotton, First Corporal.
W. B. McKenzie, Second Corporal.
M. S. Dollins, Third Corporal.
T. H. Clark, Fourth Corporal.

PRIVATES.

Ashley J. R.
Armstrong, Jesse.
Armstrong, Thomas.
Armstrong, William.
Ashby, Elias.
Brewer, J. R.
Brown, J. B.
Bell, J. N.
Borough, G. W.

Ingle, W. H.
Jolly, Jas.
King, J. D.
King, Jeff.
Leonard, J. W.
McKenzie, John.
Moore, M. R.
Moore, J. F.
Moore, J. A. F.

Broadaway, Jesse.
Clift, A. P.
Cunningham, John.
Carrigan, C. H.
Crenshaw, W. T.
Colter, F. M.
Curtis, T. H.
Cummings, Henry.
Epps, J. G.
Epps, J. N.
Freeman, A. C.
Freeman, W. J.
Fox, R. F.
Fincher, J. W.
Gibson, W. H.
Green, G. A. N.
Hall, W. C.
Hall, Richard.
Hall, C. C.
Hale, G. W.
Hamby, L.
Hudson, H. F.
Hudson, W. B.
Hudson, J. L.
Headricks, J. B.
Harrison, J. G.
Hines, Joe.

Mills, J. E.
Miller, Chas.
Morris, Amos.
Pylant, M. F.
Pearson, James.
Pylant, G. A. F.
Prosser, W. D.
Reece, J.
Rives, T. J.
Robinson, T. J.
Sisk, John.
Smith, G. W.
Small, L. P. M.
Sullivan, J. W.
Smith, W. M.
Tucker, D. (Chaplain).
Thompson, Wm.
Thompson, David.
Thompson, Patrick.
Wells, Isom.
Wells, T. J.
Waid, W. L.
Wright, M. J.
Willet, John.
Yant, T. A.
Yant, M. P.

THRASH'S COMPANY (H).

[At the reorganization, —— Moore, the original Captain of the company, was elected Lieutenant-Colonel, and W. J. Thrash was elected Captain.]

OFFICERS.

W. J. THRASH, Captain.

CHEAT MOUNTAIN.

WILLIAM BONNER, JR., First Lieutenant.
W. L. SHOFNER, Second Lieutenant.
T. H. FREEMAN, Third Lieutenant.
G. W. WAGGONER, First Sergeant.
J. N. SULLIVAN, Second Sergeant.
A. H. BOONE, Third Sergeant.
J. Y. REESE, Fourth Sergeant.
M. B. SHORES, Fifth Sergeant.
R. F. STEGALL, First Corporal.
W. H. HOLMAN, Second Corporal.
J. F. WHITAKER, Third Corporal.
M. L. MEAD, Fourth Corporal.

PRIVATES.

Broughton, Jo.
Bright, J. C.
Blackwell, W. A.
Blackwell, J. E.
Brown, Thos.
Boone, H. L. W.
Brady, Alex.
Boaz, R. M.
Carrigan, W. H.
Carrigan, J. S.
Call, Jo.
Clark, J. C.
Clark, W. T.
Carter, A. M.
Cook, Stephen.
Davidson, L. W.
Davidson, W. P.
Dean, M. M.
Duff, J. H. C.
Daniel, G. D.
Eslick, John.
Eaton, J. A.

Mooney, J. S.
McAfee, A. A.
McLean, J. D.
Mills, J. F. M.
Moorhead, R. A.
Moorhead, J. L.
Miller, G. F.
Mitchell, P. Y.
Nevels, Wm.
Ousley, E. M.
Parker, J. B.
Parks, Aaron.
Parks, Joel.
Parks, E. T.
Pearson, James.
Pitts, J. C.
Pitts, J. A.
Raby, P. A.
Raby, J. R.
Rives, B. H.
Rainey, J. C.
Renager, Calvin.

Foister, J. V.
Foister, N. S.
Franklin, W. M.
Farrar, L. A.
Glidewell, Enoch
Glidewell, Aaron.
George, H. P.
George, D. S.
Gattis, Riley
Gattis, J. V.
Gattis, G. W.
Hurt, W. B.
Hague, J. C.
Honey, Eb.
Honey, Jas.
Hatchell, James.
James, R. G.
James, P. M.
Johnson, Stephen.
King, J. J.
Lester, Dr. G. B.
Logan, G. C.
Leftwich, L. B.
Lee, A. H.
Lipscomb, H. D.
Montgomery, W. M.
Morgan, B. D.
Morgan, J. C.
Martin, W. H.
Martin, W. C.

Renager, W. F.
Robertson, J. M.
Robertson, Dr. W. H.
Rutledge, W. A.
Seals, W. D.
Seals, J. S.
Shofner, Wilson L.
Shofner, C. C.
Shofner, N. M.
Sebastain, W. H.
Snelling, G. W.
Street, G. W.
Street, Asa.
Stacy, J. P.
Stegall, J. B.
Sullenger, Jas.
Tolley, J. D.
Thomison, J. B.
Waggoner, D. J.
Waggoner, G. A.
Waggoner, F. M.
Waggoner, G. H.
Waggoner, D. N.
Whitaker, M. D. L.
Whitaker, L. J.
Whitman, J. W.
Whitman, E. D.
Wilson, J. M. D.
Woodard, W. A.
Yates, E. W.

There was also one company from Marshall county, Tennessee, and the following is a list of the officers and men of that company:

BRYANT'S COMPANY (A.)

OFFICERS.

J. L. Bryant, Captain.
J. P. Holland, First Lieutenant.
B. B. Bowers, Second Lieutenant.
T. F. Brooks, Third Lieutenant.
T. E. Russell, Orderly Sergeant.

PRIVATES.

Andrews, W. C.
Bethune, D. A.
Bethune, W. M.
Biggers, J. F.
Biggers, J. W.
Biggers, R. W.
Blackwell, W. T.
Brents, T. E.
Brooks, J. S.
Busset, Wiles.
Butler, J. R.
Carrier, W. L.
Cauley, Monroe.
Cauler, Joe.
Causby, G. W.,
Collins, J. B.
Collins, Jones.
Crabtree, George.
Darnell, J. H.
Dodd, Joel.
Dodd, W. S.
Largen, Milton.
Largen, R. H.
Luna, J. M.
Luna, M. V.
Luna, R. H.
Luna, William.
Malone, E.
Malone, W. A.
Maulden, H. N.
Meadows, A. M.
Morris, J. A.
McAfee, J. M.
McCrory, J. A.
McCrory, R. J.
McCrory, W. H.
Nichols, J. M.
Patterson, A. J.
Peach, W. H.
Pearson, W. H.
Petty, M.
Pyles, H. M.

Dyer, J. D.
Foster, George.
Franklin, Thomas.
Gulley, W. F.
Haislip, J.
Haislip, J. H.
Haislip, J. W.
Hill, O. P.
Hitchman, J. N.
Hitchman, W. L.
Hogan, D. P.
Hogan, J. A.

Rambo, E. F.
Russell, G. W.
Sanders, J. C.
Shaw, R. A.
Shaw, R. J.
Shaw, W. J.
Stilwell, J.
Tally, D. E.
Tally, J. J.
Tally, J. N.
Tally, P. H.
Troop, J. G.

Wakefield, J. F. W.

The other five companies of the regiment were made up in, and were from, the counties as follows; the names of the captains of each company only being given, as it has been impossible for us, to our great regret, to obtain lists of the other officers and men.

There were two companies from Overton county, Tennessee—Company "D" and Company "F." Company "D" was commanded by D. C. Miers, and Company "F" by Tim S. McHenry. Two companies were from Jackson county, Tennessee—Company "E," commanded by James Armstrong, and Company "K" by William Gore. One company from Smith county, Company "I," commanded by James Burford.

We trust we may be pardoned for going back a few steps and recalling the attending scenes and excitement of the days of 1861, and during the formation of these companies. In doing this we feel confident that in a great measure we will illustrate the ludicrous ideas and notions prevailing all over this country at that time, and sample out, in small patterns, the complete stock of ignorance of war, in all its appalling phases and all its devastation and death, on hand and in stock among us. But when we reflect that, as a people, we knew nothing but the blessings of peace, the full and complete enjoyment of our rights under a republican form of government, a reason for our ignorance may be found and a satisfactory explanation given.

FORMATION OF THE EIGHTH REGIMENT.

Early in the spring of 1861, and after the fall of Fort Sumter, and the call of President Lincoln for troops from Tennessee, war was the only thing talked of or discussed in this country. Old gray-haired men, devoted wives, sisters and mothers talked of war until the whole atmosphere was full of it. To look back over the events of those days, it seems strange now how rapidly public sentiment has changed.

In the month of February of that year, the question of secession—certain war—was submitted to the people of Tennessee for a popular vote, and for ratification on the one hand or rejection on the other, and the people decided against secession at the ballot-box by a majority of over sixty thousand; but in the month of May following to publicly oppose secession, either as a principle or as an expediency, was almost certain political martyrdom, and social ostracism was by no means doubtful or uncertain. Little tow-headed boys were shouting the battle-whoop from every cabin in the country. So great was this feeling that almost every blacksmith in the land began to make, out of old saws, and indeed any metal they could hammer down to an edge, large, ugly, ill-shaped Bowie knives. As an adjunct to this method of manufacturing "war cutlery," the old-fashioned country grindstones were put into motion, to whet and grind up these huge instruments to a sharp point and edge.

We have seen little "runts" of men, with as many as two of these knives, encased in rough scabbards, belted around them, and armed to the teeth, thus they made the eternal hills around them resound with their cries for war. They imagined that in the beginning there would be nothing but a hand-to-hand fight, and with these weapons they would successfully defend their country, their homes and their firesides. The truth is, along about this time, too many of us had been taught by a few "fanatical" leaders that one southern man could whip at least five men from the North. Sectionalism had chrystalized until the fatal "Mason and Dixon's line" was too often looked upon as a sort of reverential division line by both sections, and the result was jealousy, embittered feelings and distrust of each other.

But underlying all this southern excitement, not to call it, in many instances, fanaticism, was a deep and righteous loyalty to the land and home of every southerner and his institutions, and no power could restrain the uprising of the people to repel an invading foe, and defend themselves from what they believed to be an unholy and unjust war.

With this prevailing sentiment in the minds of the people, meetings were often held in the various neighborhoods, and on these occasions there was no deficiency in the number of speakers, for what was wanting in quality was made up in quantity. On some of these occasions, we remember well to have heard men try to make war speeches who never before or since lifted their voices in strains of eloquent patriotism to stir the souls of their countrymen. The "Vandal hordes" of the North, their great enmity to the South, their love for the negro, and their desire and purpose to elevate him to the level of the people of the South, or their intention to pull the people of the South down to his level, were presented in glowing colors, and in many high sounding words. Our rights in the territories and the ruinous results to the South of the doctrine of "Squatter Sovereignty," and many other kindred subjects, were taught us by the political chiefs and sachems of that day and time. How near some of these issues have been accomplished by the results of the war we will not discuss.

But, so pregnant was the air filled with some of these wild infatuations, that men, women and children of all ages, sizes and colors, went out to these meetings, and gladly, it seemed, joined in the general enthusiasm of the country. Soon, under this state of excitement, with war declared, the North against the South, companies began to be organized. At the beginning, everybody wished to go and fight the "Yankees." "Just let me to 'em," was the impatient utterance of the land at that time. On many occasions, when a call was made for volunteers, young ladies would walk out and fall into line, and this was a signal for all men present to fall in. With this element of wild fire sweeping over the country, is it at all strange or beyond proper explanation, that the old men, the middle-aged men, and young men of the country rushed into the ranks of the Confederate army, not knowing or dreaming what awaited them? It is, however, true, with all advantages against them, with no great stores of war implements, with no money and no credit, with two thousand miles of defenseless coast, and without a navy, when in the fight once, they fought as never men fought before. But it must not be supposed for a moment that this sentiment of fight and war did not exist in all classes of society. The most refined and intelligent ladies of the country eagerly participated in these meetings, and to them and their influence must be awarded much of the praise for the prompt manner in which the men all over the country flew to arms to repel invasion.

Illustrating to some extent the manner of those days, we here mention that at the organization of Higgins' Company of the Eighth Regiment, on Norris Creek, Lincoln county, Tennessee, the ladies of the vicinity made and presented to the company, at its organization, a beautiful large flag, the presentation being made just a few days before its departure, by Miss Sallie Landess, who delivered on the occasion the following eloquent and stirring address :

Gentlemen of the Norris Creek Guards:

The great chronicler of events is now recording in characters of blood this epoch in our country's history ; and why should the record be written in a nation's blood ? Dare any one to stigmatize you, the sons of Tennessee, as lawless desperadoes, that would gloat with demoniac rejoicings over a brother's fate sealed with blood ! Is there a blemish upon the fair escutcheon of the fame of the " Volunteer State," that would justify the ignominious accusation that you are not a peace-loving and law abiding people, ready at all times to pay homage to the shrine of the constitution of your fathers? Have your accusers (if any there be) forgotten how, in the struggle for independence, your fathers braved death on the heights of King's Mountain? Have the glories achieved by the hero of the Hermitage, and his gallant followers upon the plains of New Orleans, been blotted from their memories? Have they ceased to remember that splendid exhibition of chivalry which led to victory at Vera Cruz, Cerro Gordo and Chepultepec, and finally enabled the American army to plant with one triumphant shout their banner upon what had been considered the impregnable battlements of the Montezumas? And, can any one suppose that you, the descendants and brothers of these intrepid warriors, whose deeds of glory are written in burnished characters upon the pages of your country's history, will be less vigilant, less watchful of your rights, your honor, your homes and friends? He who would stultify himself with this belief, has studied to little purpose southern chivalry.

The once quiet and happy homes of our "Sunny South" are invaded by the myrmidons of the Black Republican usurper of the North. They insolently demand our homes. They would desecrate our altars and overthrow our institutions. They haughtily bid us to surrender the graves of our Washington, Jefferson, Madison and Jackson, to be trampled over with fiendish delight by the revilers of all that is sacred and holy.

Your defiant, yet noble, answer to this menace is clearly expressed in the indignant flash of those cloudless eyes. The heritage is ours; God gave it to our fathers. Beware who touches! for our arms can never be manacled by the chains of political despotism, more oppressive than Draco's bloody laws, that hung the Athenian government in mourning. And now, when they would enforce their impious designs, your are buckling on your armor to resist the unholy crusade. You have espoused a cause untarnished by a stain of reproach or ambition, else these, your mothers, wives and sisters, would not be here to-day to animate you with approving smiles and cheering words.

As a testimonial of their confidence in your prowess and your inflexible determination to maintain the liberties of yourselves, your children and your kindred, or perish upon the ensanguined fields of war, I, in behalf of the ladies of Norris Creek, present you with this flag, and with it we invoke the blessings of God upon you. Armed, as you are, with right, justice and approving conscience—weapons more potent than bristling bayonets and death-dealing cannons—we fear not that it will ever trail in the dust of dishonor. When its silken folds float over you, let it admonish you that whether in the mists of morning, in the shimmering noontide, or when the earth is shrouded in its pall of darkness, there are orisons ascending in your behalf from the hearts of those who have trusted to your keeping this token of reliance on your valor. When upon the tented field, 'mid the music of war, the thunder of battle raging around you, remember that your mothers and wives, sisters and children, liberty and Christianity, are the trophies for your struggle. Do this, and when the smoke of each terrific conflict shall have been borne from the field, the battlements of victory will be crowned with your standard. Then, while

"The trumpet is sounding from mountain to shore,
Your swords and your lances must slumber no more.
Fling forth to the sunlight your banner on high,
Inscribed with the watchword, 'We conquer or die!'
Go forth in the pathway your fathers have trod;
You, too, fight for freedom—your Captain is God.
Their blood in your veins, with their honors you vie,
Their's, too, was the watchword, 'We conquer or die.'
March on to the battle-field, there to do or to dare,
With shoulder to shoulder, all danger to share,
And let your proud watchword spring up to the sky,
'Till the blue arch re-echoes, 'We conquer or die.'
Press forward undaunted, nor think of retreat,
The enemy's host on the threshold to meet;
Strike firm, 'till the foemen before you shall fly,
Appalled by your watchword, 'We conquer or die.'"

While there were many ludicrous things done, as they now seem to us at this day and time, that an intelligent devotion and true patriotism to the "Southland" lay at the bottom of all that was done and said, none can question.

For instance, as the time approached for our departure, the devoted wives, sisters and mothers began to pack up boxes and trunks full of clothing and bed-quilts, and some good things to eat, and by the time the four Lincoln county companies got ready to start off, a wagon was required to each man to haul his baggage. We soon found that the baggage business was not in accord with the life of a soldier, and had to be for nothing held.

By the last of May, 1861, several companies had been organized in Lincoln county, and indeed in all the surrounding counties, and some had left for the field of conflict. The four Lincoln county companies of the Eighth Regiment left the depot at Fayetteville, on the 14th day of May, 1861, and on the same day landed at Camp Harris, in Franklin county, Tenn., and on the 17th of the same month were mustered into the service of the State by Col. D. R. Smythe, of Lincoln county. Here we were supplied with our camp equipage, consisting chiefly of tin-cups, frying-pans and domestic tent cloths, all of which we regarded with much indifference, for we were out after "Yankees" and blood, and not the good things of this world. Here we remained until the 23d of May, when we received orders to go to Camp Trousdale, in Sumner county, Tenn. On the 24th we found ourselves quartered at this camp.

On the 29th the Eighth Tennessee Regiment, composed

of the companies heretofore referred to, was organized, and the following regimental officers were elected, viz.:

Colonel—Alfred S. Fulton, Fayetteville, Lincoln county, Tenn.
Lieutenant-Colonel—W. Lawson Moore, Mulberry, Lincoln county, Tenn.
Major—W. H. Botts, Jackson county, Tenn.
Adjutant—Chris. C. McKinney, Petersburg, Lincoln county, Tenn.
Surgeon—Dr. G. W. Gray, Carthage, Smith county, Tenn.
Assistant Surgeon—Dr. G. B. Lester, Charity, Lincoln county, Tenn.
Quartermaster—L. W. Oglesby, Overton county, Tenn.
Commissary—Al. Ewing, Nashville, Davidson county, Tenn.
Chaplain—David Tucker, Norris Creek, Lincoln county, Tenn.
Drum Major—R. A. Cox, Jackson county, Tenn.

Thus we were officered, and thus we began the great task before us. We shall never forget the first dress parade or drill of the regiment after its organization.

Our upper county companies had no advantage of us in either dress, equipage or military discipline. They, too, had caught the big knife fever, and supported about two apiece, belted around in true soldier-like style. But they were all good men, kind and gallant. No set of men thrown together as strangers in times like those ever passed through more trying scenes more pleasantly together than did this organization of troops. At our first meeting, and after briefly intermingling with each other, we soon found a common cause had formed within us a common feeling, and no trouble ever arose among any of the men or companies. The officers and men from Overton, Jackson and Smith counties were intelligent and hospitable people, and many warm ties of friendship were formed among the men that will follow each to his grave. Captains Miers, Burford, Gore, McHenry, Lieutenants Wright, Bradley, Cullom, the Messrs. Davis, Cox, and, in fact all, are remembered with kindness by the Lincoln county boys.

But of all the dirty, ragged soldiers ever seen at that age of the world, none surpassed the Eighth Regiment! We wore all sorts of clothing, all sorts of hats and caps. Our dress ranged from the butternut jeans up to the finest article of French cloth, the butternut, however, largely predominating. Our large, bloody-looking knives were the only things possessing much similarity, and a failure to have one of these pieces of war cutlery dangling at your side was almost a certain sign of weakness in the knees. By this time the weather was growing warm, and often some of the boys would drill barefooted and without coats. And what a motley looking line of old men, middle-aged men and young men was here presented! Men from plow handles, out of workshops, men who never before had seen a regiment of soldiers in line, and who knew as little about war as infants; men who, flattering themselves that each was an invincible Hercules, and could slay his allotted five Yankees within the next ensuing sixty days and return home to his family, with his country saved, were then in the full enjoyment of a blissful ignorance.

As still higher evidence of the devotion and patriotism of the country, each company had its flag, and when a speech was made to us (and about that time they averaged about three per day), the flags were pointed to in the midst of some lofty flights of eloquence, and the boys, with their huge knives gleaming in the sunbeams, would make the "welkin ring" and each speaker felt himself covered all over with glory. This was the foretaste and the *sweet*.

As matters of interest, and giving a faithful account of just what existed and what was going on, we insert the following letters, written from Camp Trousdale. This was written by David Tucker, Chaplain of the Eighth Regiment:

From the Fayetteville Observer.

CAMP TROUSDALE, TENN., May 31, 1861.

MR. N. O. WALLACE: Now having a few moments to spare, I with pleasure, amid the noise and bustle of camp, drop you a few lines for publication, if you think proper, that the good people of Lincoln county may know how we are getting along, and what we are doing.

The boys are all well with few exceptions, and in good spirits. Some are complaining and have been quite sick, which is not uncommon in camps, especially with those who have not been used to exposure and act imprudently. I have just been around this morning to see the sick, and found them all improving. I think when we all become seasoned to camp life, and regular in our habits, we will do well.

We formed one regiment and elected our officers last Wednesday. We elected A. S. Fulton, of Fayetteville, Lincoln county, commanding Colonel; William Lawson Moore, of Mulberry, Lincoln county, Lieutenant-Colonel; Mr. Botts, of Jackson county, Major. Mr. Botts was a private in Captain Gore's company. We have good officers—men upon whom we can rely.

It was agreed upon before we held our election that Lincoln county should have the two first offices and Jackson county the third. The other officers of the regiment will be filled out by the companies from other counties, except such as our Colonel has the power to fill by appointment.

I now give you the county, title of company, the name of each captain as positioned in regiment, and number of men, rank and file:

Jackson county, "Gainesboro Invincibles," Capt. Gore, number of men, 99.

Jackson county, "Celina Invincibles," Capt. Armstrong, number of men, 80.

Marshall county, "New Hope Volunteers," Capt. Bryant, number of men, 98.

Lincoln county, "Camargo Guards," Capt. McKinney, number of men, 100.

Lincoln county, "Norris Creek Guards," Capt. Higgins, number of men, 78.

Lincoln county, "Mulberry Riflemen," Capt. Moore, number of men, 104.

Lincoln county, "Petersburg Sharp-shooters," Capt. Hall, number of men, 78.

Smith county, "Dixon Springs Guards," Capt. Burford, number of men, 62.

Overton county, "Overton Guards," Capt. Miers, number of men, 99.

Overton county, "Overton Blues," Capt. McHenry, number of men, 91.

We make quite a show when we meet on the field. Our coming together seems to animate us; we can perform much better. We have no schisms in our regiment—all get along smoothly. It would do you good to see the unanimity of feeling existing among the boys, the variety of amusements in which they engage, the droll expressions they use, the appellations they bear. Each mess or family has a Mary, Lucy, Nancy, etc., and many regulations in the domestic circle which are amusing. It would surprise you to see the improvement they have made in the culinary art. They are getting to be excellent cooks, learning how to fix up a variety of eatables which add much to the table and give us a relish for our food. I would just say to our good friends of Norris Creek that we are under lasting obligations to them for the nice lot of provisions which they sent us last week. The boys highly appreciate your kindness. We saved those luxuries received from you for Sunday. We had quite a feast, I assure you; invited our friends to dine with us, embracing several preachers. All seemed to enjoy it very much, and joined with us in eulogising the good and patriotic women of Old Lincoln.

Bros. Hardin, Rutledge and myself held prayer meeting on Saturday night in camp, and had a pleasant time. Your humble servant preached Sunday, at 10 o'clock A. M., and Brother Hardin at 3 P. M. We had a social prayer-meeting at candle-lighting, Bros. Boideston, Hardin and Rutledge joining with us. Bro. Rutledge conducted the services.

I am resolved to do all I can for our Lincoln county boys, and those with whom we are associated. I enter this campaign, not with the expectation of gaining honor nor making money, but will be satisfied if we can maintain our independence, preserve our liberties and those sacred institutions that our forefathers bequeathed to us and our posterity, without which life would be a burden and afford no enjoyment. God forbid that our happy Columbia, the Sunny South, should ever be demolished and subdued by Northern fanatics.

Yours respectfully, DAVID TUCKER.

As appropriate, we also insert a letter written from the

same place, and about the same time, by G. W. Higgins, Captain of Company "G," of the Eighth Regiment:

From the Fayetteville Observer.

CAMP TROUSDALE, TENN., June 28, 1861.

DEAR WALLACE—As you have had a respite for a week from the task of setting type for "Volunteer letters," I have concluded to drop you a few lines."

I would have written to you last week, but expected to be ordered home on a recruiting expedition; but while I was rejoicing over the pleasure of spending a week with my dear friends in old Lincoln, an order came to hold ourselves in readiness to march at an hour's notice. Thus, in the short space of an hour, I felt joys the most ecstatic, and then—suffered disappointment the most poignant. Who knows the sacredness of friendship's ties 'till cut aloof from the association of friends? Who can estimate the intense suffering the human heart is heir to, 'till separated from all (save honor) that makes life dear? Who can feel the rapture, the happiness real, that lifts our thoughts from earth to heaven, but the poor soldier, when he is about to be granted that highest boon to him—a furlough to visit his loved ones? But this is not all that saddens me. My company, which was small at first, has been reduced on account of discharges, promotions, sickness, etc., to hardly a corporal's guard. I know full well that I could in one week bring up recruits enough to not only fill up the vacancies, but to increase my company from that of a minimum to that of a maximum size.

Details are not made from companies according to their relative strength, but each company must furnish an equal number of men for guard and fatigue duty. This is hard work on a small company. A minimum company of 76 men must do the same labor as a maximum company of 104 men. For instance, I have absent sick, 5; present sick, 10; attendants on sick, 2; discharged, 1 (E. A. Ashley); promoted, 1 (Rev. David Tucker, Chaplain); all which taken from my original 78, leaves me 53 men, rank and file.

Now, friend Wallace, I must have 20 or 25 men. I can furnish them plenty of good, wholesome food and the necessary clothing, besides an equal participation in the glory of fighting for the rights handed down to us by our fathers. Can you do anything towards getting them for me? I would be pleased to have them forthwith.

Approving the bold and manly stand that Gov. Jackson, of Missouri, has taken, I think it our duty to go to his assistance; nor would I be surprised if we did go, as the marching order has not yet been canceled.

For fear the report of the sick might alarm some of the good mothers, I will say there is not a case in the company considered dangerous. We have several cases of measles, and though they have not the soothing hands and consoling words of wife, mother or sister, they have the best attention from their comrades in arms. Upon the whole, we are getting along very well, and in good spirits, etc. Yours truly,

G. W. H., Co. "G."

We remained at Camp Trousdale for some time, drilling and learning the arts of war, (if there be such things), and of camp life. In other words, we were gradually undergoing the not altogether pleasant transformation of the life of a citizen to the life of a soldier.

The change of diet and habits of life were rapidly telling on us. The measles soon made their appearance in camps, and in some companies and regiments made sad havoc of many noble young men, and kind fathers and husbands; and it became common talk that it looked like none but the best of men were dying, or even got sick.

The hardened old *cupes*, or the swearing old fellows, who would walk a mile to steal a sheep, or rob a hen-roost, seemed to be utterly beyond the ravages of all diseases. However this may be, many men, full of life and high expectations for the future, died. John Cunningham, of Higgins' Company, and P. H. Tally, of Bryant's Company, passed under the great cloud of death, while yet in their full manhood and usefulness, after a few days' sickness. Perhaps, a more inexperienced set of men were never organized into one body than that of the Eighth Regiment. Nearly every man, in the ranks at least, knew nothing but hard labor, and any discipline was a difficult matter for them to learn. They knew exactly how to manage a plow, wield an axe, push a plane, or direct a hammer, and were splendid shots with the rifle; but to level themselves down to obedience, tactics and rigid military discipline, was almost impossible; and this important fact was often overlooked by some swell-headed officers in command.

Man, at best, is but a creature of lessons, habit and thought, and time and application have their work to perform on him before he can adapt himself to various kinds of life, and discharge faithfully the various duties incident to different spheres in life. Hence, we have often thought that it was the work of some hidden power, that these men should be chosen as raw materials, to discharge the task they were soon to undertake.

But here we must give a brief synopsis of the Sixteenth Regiment of Tennessee Volunteers, which was also organized at Camp Trousdale, and about the same time the Eighth was.

FORMATION OF THE SIXTEENTH REGIMENT OF TENNESSEE VOLUNTEERS.

Colonel—John H. Savage, McMinnville, Tenn.
Lieutenant Colonel—Thomas B. Murray.
Major—Jo. H. Goodbar.
Adjutant—George Marchbanks.
Commissary—James Glasscock.
Quarter Master—G. R. Campbell.
Surgeon—J. T. Reid.
Assistant Surgeon—C. K. Mauzy.
Chaplain—J. R. Poindexter.

The following is a list of the captains of the ten companies composing this regiment, and we much regret we cannot avail ourselves of other information concerning the gallant men of this regiment, but we are advised not to do so at present, as this matter is in the hands of another person, who will, no doubt, do them justice:

First Captain—L. N. Savage, DeKalb county, Tenn.
Second Captain—P. C. Shields, DeKalb county, Tenn.
Third Captain—D. T. Brown, White county, Tenn.
Fourth Captain—C. C. Brewer, Coffee county, Tenn.
Fifth Captain—J. J. Womack, Warren county, Tenn.
Sixth Captain—L. H. Meadows, Warren county, Tenn.
Seventh Captain—D. M. Donnel, Warren county, Tenn.
Eighth Captain—P. H. Coffee, Warren county, Tenn.
Ninth Captain—H. York, Van Buren county, Tenn.
Tenth Captain—H. H. Dillard, Putnam county, Tenn.

We are at a loss to know exactly when the Brigade (Donelson's) was formed, but it was after we reached Virginia, in July, 1861. On the 20th of July, 1861, the two regiments received orders to cook three days' rations, and to pack up, the evening of the same day, and report at the depot.

So far as the soldiers in the ranks were concerned, they did not know whether they were to go to Halifax, Richmond, or Pluto's dominions; and, with many of them, it made but little difference. The boys acted with much promptness and eagerness in their preparations, but with our original enthusiasm somewhat cooled down; for, by this time, we all began to realize that going to war was not exactly just what we thought it would be, and we were gradually learning that we were not sailing through the skies of war "on flowery beds of ease."

Enough, however, was whispered around for us to find out we were not going back home. We spent a miserable night waiting at the depot for transportation, and it was near daylight on the morning of the 21st, before we got started, and about two or three o'clock in the evening, we landed in the city of Nashville, and the citizens there treated us very kindly. In marching through the city, and on our line of march from the Louisville depot to the Chattanooga depot, the front doors were filled with people waving handkerchiefs, and many standing at their front gates with water, some with something to eat, which was handed to us as we passed. We remember an old gentleman by the name of Hill, on Church street, who stood out at his gate and invited the boys to go in and get them something to eat; and many a poor ragged, hungry soldier walked right in and was bountifully fed from his table. We do not know what became of him or his good wife, or on what side he eventually fell; but the gratitude of many poor "Rebs" he, no doubt, won on that day. Other citizens of the city did the same thing, but we can not remember their names. Late that night, we left in some box-cars for Chattanooga, the officers and negro cooks being furnished with a coach to ride in, and about 8 o'clock next morning landed in Chattanooga. Chattanooga at that time was anything but a city of houses. The depot building, the mud, the gnats, the mosquitoes, the frogs, and a few wild dirt-dauber looking people, were about all we encountered here. Still profoundly ignorant of our destination, we left in the evening for Knoxville. After a tiresome, tedious, sleepless and tasteless night spent on the train, we landed at Knoxville almost exhausted, as we thought. The people of that place received us kindly. Indeed, they, to our astonishment, were more alive, and dispensed their charities among us more freely, if possible, than any people we had met. Their doors were thrown wide open, and many an ugly, dirty looking Confederate soldier partook of their hospitalities. The question was frequently asked, "How can this be, here in the home of Brownlow?" But it was true. We remember Mrs. Whitsett and the Morrow family, who did much for us, especially among our sick. Here we remained until Wednesday morning without unloading our equipage from the box-cars. The boys, of course, took in the city, many of them having never been that far from home before. From Knoxville we learned we had been ordered on to Bristol; and just as the train was backing out to start for that point, many of us witnessed a most shocking accident. A man by the name of Law, a member of Miers' Company, fell on the track from the rear end of the car, and the wheels passed over his leg, cutting it completely off, and the man, after lingering a few days in great pain and agony, died. This, while amounting to but little in war, was not calculated to inspire us with much courage, for along about this time you could occasionally hear some fellow say, " I wish I was at home." But off we went, giving, as the train pulled out, three hearty cheers for the good people of Knoxville.. The order seemed to be to travel about five miles and stop about five hours.

Stop, stop, was indulged in until the boys became impatient and unmanageable. At last we landed at Bristol, on Friday morning, the 26th of July. We unloaded, moved out about one mile west of the place, erected our tents, got up some nice clean straw for beds, began to wash our clothing, and were cooking something to eat, when orders came to pack up and report at the depot in one hour. This we did, but with much confusion, interspersed with many d—s, such as raw soldiers could get up and shoot off on such occasions.

Tired, sleepy and hungry, we reported back at the depot, and were told we had been ordered to Lynchburg, Va. On the train once more, we soon moved out from Bristol for Lynchburg. After traveling about fifteen miles that night, cooped up in a lot of old box cars, the weather having become very warm, we were stopped, as usual. After a stay here of about two hours, the train began to move backward. Back and back it went until, to the disgust and surprise of every one, we found ourselves again at the depot at Bristol.

We again unloaded and made our way out, as best we could, to our first camping ground, where some fell down to sleep, some began to cook, and not a few engaged in short discourses in improved profanity.

Just as the entire command was passing into a sound slumber, known only to a wearied soldier, orders came to pack up and report at the depot at six o'clock that morning. This gave us but a short time to cook some scanty rations, and we again reported for the trip, but occasionally you, if a close listener, might have heard some fellow say away down in his stomach, "I'm getting darned tired of this here foolishness."

On the 29th of July we reached the city of Lynchburg, unloaded our box-cars, marched through the town and went into camp about one mile from the city. As usual, the boys soon spread themselves over the city, and had it down to a fine point, for we soon found our advent into the place had failed to arouse any enthusiasm or attract any attention. The tobacco houses and the vast number of filthy looking negroes at work in them, were about the only objects to attract our attention, and hence matters were about even with us all around. On the 31st we left the old nasty looking city of Lynchburg, and were told we were going to Charlottesville, and from there perhaps to the devil.

We must here mention that the great battle of Manassas had been fought just a few days before, and the whole army was flushed with the joy and enthusiasm of that victory. This news was a great stimulus to the men, and inspired them with renewed confidence.

We all thought we were soon to join that part of the army that had just won the great victory in a great battle, and all were anxious to go out, and old muskets for the first time were rubbed up and brightened, and our great knives were whetted up and put in good cutting order. We are confident that up to this time not one of us had ever fired a musket at any living man, or heard the roar of cannon. We know none of us had, as yet, seen a "Yankee" in full uniform, dead or living.

With that complete stock of war ignorance on hand, is it any wonder we should "*pant*" for a fight like a deer for water after a long chase?

It has been said that "ignorance is bliss," and whether true or not, we are confident that ignorance of a battle among men often tends to uphold and give moving power to their courage and bravery. We reached Charlottesville on the first day of August. Here we saw many wounded Confederate soldiers.

The people here were fully aroused and seemed to appreciate the condition of the issues around them. The fine large college building was filled with sick and wounded men, and here we had a chance to witness for the first time some of the fruits or results of war.

We did not remain long at this place, but as yet we did not know where we were to go, what duties to perform, or what might be assigned to us.

On the second day of August we landed in Staunton, Va. After taking just time enough to unload our baggage from the box-cars, arrange our knapsacks, cartridge boxes, canteens and some other minor appurtenances, we started out on foot to some place to this deponent unknown.

After our long and tedious journey in the cars, every man was delighted with the chance of marching on foot, and exercising himself in such way as to regain his activity and strength, his appetite needing little or no attention. The weather was now indeed oppressively warm; yet, gradually learning how to adapt ourselves to the new order of things, we moved out with high hopes, if not bright ones, with our bosoms full of enthusiasm, (not quite so full as they had been), not knowing or caring whither we went. Soon we began to realize the fact that we were approaching the mountains of Northwest Virginia; but what was a mountain to a soldier from Middle Tennessee? On we went with all the glee and mirth of a lot of men just let out of a pen, and at night we found ourselves at Buffalo Gap. On the next day we marched to a place called Bell Valley, or Pine Grove, and camped during that night. The next day, which was Sunday, and the 4th of the month, we moved onward still, and up hills and down valleys, and came to and crossed Calf Pasture river, and that night went into camps on its banks.

On Monday, the fifth day of August, we crossed the Alleghany Mountains. From the top of these mountains we had a most excellent and magnificent view of the surrounding country. To say that the sight before us was grand, sublime and panoramic, is giving a feeble outline of the magnificence and beauty spread out before us. Mountain after mountain seemed rolled out in perfect order, and placed one alongside of the other in the most systematic manner, and finished up in the highest style and grandeur of nature's God; and like ocean waves in the distance, rolling one after the other, filled the beholder with such feelings of admiration as no language can fairly describe. It seemed as though the great God of nature had been bestowing His richest garlands of beauty with partial distinction on these everlasting and majestic mountains. Here we beheld the great handiwork of omnipotent power. Great and grand as this view was, we here looked upon mere pigmies, compared with those reserved for us to behold and traverse in the near future.

On the evening of the 5th, we landed at Warm Springs, in Pocahontas county, Va., and there camped for the night. This wonder was another new chapter in the lives of these Tennessee troops. The sight of water spontaneously gushing up out of the earth warm enough to emit a constant, warm and moist vapor, was such a phenomenon that we could not exactly comprehend it, and hence the men began to theorize on the subject as only men in the army can theorize on any obtuse problem or subject. Some regarded these pools of warm water as the pools of Siloam, changed over into this country by some miraculous omnipotent power from the land of the old Jerusalem, while others insisted that the "Old Boy," who rules the dominions below with absolute and despotic power, had run up a few spouts from his quarters, to give to mankind a little warning or taste of what he was reserving for them in the future; while not a few held that these warm evidences plainly established the fact that the devil had a finger in the works of nature, as he had an index finger in the social and religious governments of mankind in general. These and various other philosophical arguments were advanced, but as a matter of curiosity alone, many of the boys disrobed and plunged in.

We confess, we found the water a little too warm, and did not enjoy it very long or often; but we know of some people in this country who ought to go there and wash themselves in that water seven times for seven days, and then we doubt if that would clean them. We soon became thoroughly conversant with this famous watering place and its surroundings, and without more, we shall pass on.

On Tuesday, the 6th, we arrived and camped at Grigg's Mills, some eighteen miles from Warm Springs, and still further into the mountains.

On the 8th, we passed through a little place called Huntersville, the capital of Pocahontas county. We found this place encompassed round about by rugged hills and mountains. It looked like a complete success as an *accident*, within itself, having, in our estimation, neither inlets nor outlets, and possessing but little, if any, vitality.

We soon ascertained that many of the people here were not friendly to the cause we had espoused, all of which had a slight tendency to make some of the boys at times aggressive and reckless, especially when pinched by hunger. Six miles beyond this place we unloaded our baggage wagons and erected our tents in regular army style, near Greenbrier river, and on a spot of earth well known and remembered by the brigade as Marlin Bottom. Here we remained for two days and nights, resting, rubbing up and washing up and overhauling our camp equipage and appurtenances generally.

We insert here a letter written by "Flint Lock" from Marlin Bottom, giving in detail some interesting information concerning the situation of affairs, and being written while all the facts and events were fresh in the mind, we ask its careful reading:

From the Fayetteville Observer.

MARLIN BOTTOM, VA., Aug. 17, 1861.

MR. EDITOR: After numberless ups and downs, (most of them "downs"), we halted at this place, called Marlin Valley, but in reality mud valley—the last place in the world, and I am of opinion we are near the jumping-off place. We had some trials getting here. We were dragged from one horse-stall to another until we arrived at Staunton, and then we footed it to this place, a distance of ninety miles, and old "Flint Lock" came very near giving up the ghost, and if it had not been for the superabundance of patriotism he had aboard, he would have caved. But I am now prepared to walk anywhere and any distance. My feet have grown out again, and the bottoms of them are so thick that the rocks and mountains of Northwestern Virginia can make no impression on them.

I have seen nothing attractive in this country but rattlesnakes, and they are eternally rattling and making a fellow jump out of his skin. One of the soldiers ahead of our regiment killed five around and one in his tent.

I have read a great deal about the romantic scenery of Northwestern Virginia, and I have come to the conclusion that the individuals who wrote such stuff never had the extraordinary pleasure of wearing their feet out to their ankles walking over the mountains to see the romantic scenery, as I did, or they wrote such stuff to gull the other people, after they had been gulled themselves.

I assert, on the honor of a man who is a long way from home, and with a good prospect of getting into battle soon, that there is no romance in Northwestern Virginia, or any scenery to be seen. I have seen one or two citizens since I have been here, and they looked like Egyptian mummies just excavated from their graves after being dead seventeen hundred years or more.

I do not wish, by any means, to convey the idea that I

am dissatisfied with the country. I am well pleased with it, and have the satisfaction of knowing that in a month from now we will be perfectly safe from the enemy, because the roads, I understand, cannot be traveled either horseback or footback, owing to the rain, snow and ice.

You will never hear from old "Flint Lock" after September 1st, until spring, for I intend to get me a jug of "tangle-foot"—or in plain words, whisky—and then enter into the torpid state in conjunction with the rattlesnakes, and hibernate 'til spring.

We have no news for we get none, and don't want any. It would do no good in this country. We are concentrating a large force here. We have Generals Lee, Donelson and Anderson, men who possess the confidence of our entire army, and you may be assured that with such leaders victory will perch upon our standard. All that we are afraid of is that the enemy will not stand and face the music.

There is some sickness, but none serious or dangerous, and I think after the boys get their hides dry once more all will be right. There was a Godsend in camps yesterday—the *Observer* came to hand and I was as glad as I could be.

Well, as Henry has dinner ready (it never takes two invitations for me) I will close.

Yours truly,   FLINT LOCK.

To give as thorough information of our condition and the country surrounding us as possible, we insert here another letter from this point, by Capt. H., and ask that it be read as a part of our story:

From the Fayetteville Observer.

MARLIN BOTTOM, GREENBRIER RIVER, POCAHONTAS CO., *six miles Southeast of Huntersville—eighty miles from the White Settlements—in the midst of the Alleghany Mountains, not far from Pluto's Dominions, knee-deep in mud, sick, and not very well myself, half starved, with no prospect of anything to eat, August* 12, 1861.

Mr. N. O. Wallace: Though not quite certain this communication will ever reach you (unless you have some communication with the "devil"), I will, nevertheless, comply with the promise made you, to acquaint you with our "office."

I regret, however, that I cannot do so, as there is no such institution as "post-office" in this *bottom*. You can, however, send this regiment a few copies of the *Observer* to Huntersville, Va. We may get them, as I have a very particular friend there, who furnished myself and three others a wagon to haul us out to camps, a distance of six miles, for the pitiful sum of seven dollars. He remarked that I might think it *high*. "O no," says I, "I am surprised that a man living in this part of the world should have any conscience at all."

I must try to give you some idea of the country we traveled over the last forty miles. I took the stage at Millboro, a depot on the Staunton & Jackson River Railroad; destination, Warm Springs, distant fifteen miles across the mountains.

Nothing of particular interest occurred during the trip. We were halted only once, and that was caused by a snake crossing the road and completely blockading it. It only stopped us for a few minutes. Going at a rapid gait it crossed the road in fifteen or twenty minutes, and we again moved on the *uneven* tenor of our way, and reached the Warm Springs about daylight the next morning. These Springs are a considerable *institution*. Some of the boys, however, were not pleased with them, under the impression that they were in too close proximity to the "old gentleman down below," or at least so near that the water was heated by the "*unquenchable fire*" *of hades*. I was nearly worn out when I reached the Springs, as I was just recovering from a severe spell of the flux. I had but twenty minutes to rest, when I again took the vehicle for Huntersville, distant twenty-six miles. If I had a foretaste of the world the preachers warn us to shun in the first trip, I certainly took the second degree in the trip from Warm Springs to Huntersville. As somebody says:

"Hills so high that by man were never trod,
Which, if you could climb, you would see your God."

Indeed, I have never, in the wildest stretches of imagination, dreamed of such a world as this. Saint Patrick must have had an eye to this country when he pronounced the curse upon the serpents of Ireland and sent them hither.

I found the boys at last—tolerably well, but very much dissatisfied. They have no cause of complaint certainly. Men who would complain at this country would make a row with the devil if they were in his quarters. They stand the mud pretty well, and feel greatly relieved when assured that it will quit raining about the 15th of October. *We officers* were informed yesterday that we could *draw* no more *rations*, but would be required to pay cash for them when we got them. Well, we can live awhile yet, for we have one dollar and fifteen cents in our company.

We are in twenty miles of the enemy, but there is an almost impassable barrier between us. There is but one pass across the mountains, which we are guarding. Why we should keep the Yankees out of this country in the mountains I cannot tell. 'Tis true we have *friends* here, because the bayonet is at their breasts, but they are *friends* through fear. As for the country: if steamboats were selling at a shilling apiece, I would not give a *gangway plank* for the whole of it.

By the bye, Wallace, I wish it distinctly understood that I am a candidate for the Confederate Congress, and will make a hobby on ceding this portion of Virginia to the Federal government, moving out the honest men if there be any (our Colonel says he thinks it very doubtful), and filling their places from East Tennessee. How long we will remain here, or to what point we will go, I know not. One thing I do know, this trip will have a moralizing influence upon us.

We have had such a foretaste of the "sufferings" described by Milton that we will try to shun that "world of woe."

But my time is out. Will write again when I get some paper. Goodbye. G<small>EO</small>. W. H., Co. "G."

P. S.—Lieut. Sullivan was out about three miles from camps, on picket duty, and had the good luck to kill a very nice "fawn," which, with some mountain artichokes, resembling Irish potatoes, made a dainty dish for a soldier. (I must not tell you that an old ewe bleated all next day for her lost lamb, and a neighbor said his potato patch had suffered a little). We are going to make Uncle "Davy" our forage master. H.

We then moved across the river and pitched tents in some woods and hills, and here we remained for several days. While here the boys were quite busy in canvassing the country around and getting acquainted with the natives, what few could be found.

These highland mountaineers seemed to be shy of us, and the result was there were not many acquaintances formed in that section of God's vineyard of America.

But, by this time, it should be observed, the men were rapidly learning how to adjust themselves to the emergencies of a soldier's life, and aptly comprehended the direct *necessities of occasions.* Completely cut off from home and home lessons and influences, and having in a great degree subjected the tender and sympathetic impulses of our natures to the more hardened and indifferent sensibilities of camp life, small things were not in our way, and stumbling blocks were seldom found.

We foraged rather extensively along through this country, and fat mountain pigs, young chickens, and potatoes and green corn, all made up a pretty good living for soldiers, as long as they lasted.

In the midst of our recuperation here, orders came for us to strike tents, load up the baggage wagons and move on, and still further up into the mountain gorges and stop at a large spring. This place we reached on the 11th day of August, after traveling about seven miles. Here we found one of the finest springs we ever saw. The water came spontaneously, and it seemed joyfully, up out of the earth in vast abundance. This place we called

CAMP EDRAY.

Here the measles again made their appearance in the regiments, and many of the men suffered greatly, and three or four of them died. And here it must be stated, the rain began to fall. Rain? Not a living member of the two regiments needs a rehearsal of those times to refresh his recollection of the rain of the country during that season. The whole surface of that country is made up of sharp or cone-shaped mountains, each seeming to contend with the other for height and ruggedness, and each apparently holding by some mystic power its own rain-clouds, which would empty themselves in torrents upon our unprotected heads every few hours. We had heard people talk about the windows of heaven being opened, and the rains descending; but here, in 1861, the mountain tops seemed to do all the raining, at least they gave control and direction to the floods. Rain, rain, rain! Mud,

mud, mud! Our camps at this time afforded a most excellent field for a missionary to get in good work, for the frequent and chosen expressions of most of the men were not of the highest type of good moral training. Here trouble was soon to begin. Short rations, thin and ragged clothing, rain, mud, water and measles, all mixed up together, did not go well, and were not calculated to increase our estimation of that country, or the work we were engaged in. The outlook here was indeed gloomy. Yet these ordeals and hardships brought to the surface many peculiar and astonishing traits of character.

There was a man whose name was Hare, a member of Gore's company, whose wife, named Nancy, out of mere curiosity or devotion to the flag of her country, or her love for her husband, had accompanied us through all these travels and marches, and remained with her husband in camps in real soldier style. She could walk equal to any soldier. She carried her own wardrobe, household and kitchen furniture; and when in camps she cooked and washed for the mess, of which she was a leading member. She was not exactly a queen, but she conducted her part of the campaign well. Small "cuss words" did not greatly interfere with her literature in animated discussion, and tobacco was often her favorite " chewing gum." However, in the army she was treated with great respect and deference by both officers and men, and she will be remembered by all of us living the remainder of our lives, as a plain, home spun, honest, devoted, but a misguided woman.

At Camp Edray we remained several days, fighting mud, rain, measles and vermin, and by the time our regular day's work was put in at this, we were generally ready to go to bed. Here our first regimental hospital was erected, and for a few days it looked like most of the regiment were going to take up their quarters in it. Along about this time there was developed in Higgins' company one of the greatest curiosities and puzzles in the army. A man by the name of Cotton began now to develop himself. He joined that company the morning it left Fayetteville. No one was able to find out any of his antecedent history. He was a good shoemaker. He was a baboon, Chinese visaged looking fellow, and could steal more chickens and more sheep and more bee-gums, and tell more lies, than any man in the army. He was entirely destitute of truth and honor, but always in a good humor, and ready for scout or forage duty. His great ambition seemed to be to plunder what few people lived in those wild and hideous looking mountains. At one time he came into camps with a large bee-gum, and swore to the officers he had bought it. The next day a lady came in looking for her bee-gum, but Cotton swore she was not the lady he paid the money to. This being settled, Cotton, after preparing a smoke, gently raised the top, and applying his smoke to make the bees go down, lifted off the top and, to his great shame and mortification, found it contained nothing but wet ashes. He deserted us shortly after this. He was shrewd, hardened and reckless, but withal a good soldier up to the time of his desertion.

We wish we could, with proper words and in some beautiful language, give a perfect description of the scenery round about Camp Edray — with all its clear, limpid springs of pure water, its lofty mountains reaching up into the clouds, but distrusting our ability, we pass on to other incidents of the campaign, leaving this work of "fancy" to others better trained in such lines of thought.

On Sunday, the 25th of August, our Chaplain, Mr. Tucker, preached us a good sermon. Having the confidence and respect of the men, he received good attention. "Prepare to meet thy God," was chosen as his text, and many ungodly and wicked men gave thoughtful attention to the solemn words. Those who never heard sermons delivered to soldiers in camp know but little of the actual character of these meetings.

The consistent and devoted Christian sits down on the ground by the side of the vilest sinner, and each give, for the time, the most anxious and profound attention. There are no "amen corners;" they use no organs or ornamental pulpits; they have no voices of mothers, wives and sisters to mingle in the songs of praise, and give them a sweetness and a power to captivate and elevate man's old, hardened, rough affections and sentiments.

Strange as it may seem, we never saw or heard of a disturbance in a worshiping audience of soldiers. Their worship is unpretentious, real and genuine. No amount of hypocrisy or deceit can be of advantage here, for all men are soon found out in camp life. Good men may fall in the battle of life, but man as he is, endowed with an intelligence and a hope which is an anchor to the soul, sure and steadfast, his life at last is not all blanks, even to himself.

FLAG PRESENTED TO THE EIGHTH TENNESSEE REGIMENT
BY THE LADIES OF FAYETTEVILLE.

On this same Sabbath day, and at dress parade, at 4 o'clock in the evening, a most magnificent and beautiful large flag was presented to the regiment by the ladies of Fayetteville. Adjutant Chris. C. McKinney unfolded it before the regiment and made a chaste and impressive little speech. It was accompanied by a letter from the Hon. Jno. M. Bright, who had been selected by the ladies to prepare the address and forward both to us. On the flag were written in large gold letters the words, *Patience, Courage, Victory.* By this time, however, the men had learned that the life of a soldier was not made up of milk, wine and honey; that its hardships, deprivations, constant toils and various burdens awakened other sentiments than mere love for such a life and its attending flatteries and cooings; but here was the evidence from tender hands and devoted hearts that we were well remembered at home, and the gift was one of love and sympathy. And the men received it with cheer after cheer for the good ladies who made and sent it to them.

We insert the letter of the Hon. John M. Bright, which accompanied the flag, and also the speech delivered by Maj. Botts at its presentation and acceptance on behalf of the regiment. The letter was read by the Adjutant, and is as follows:

Soldiers of the Eighth Regiment of Tennessee Volunteers:

I am commissioned by the ladies of Lincoln county to present to you this beautiful banner. You will be pleased to accept it as a token of their especial sympathy and regard for you as soldiers, and as an expression of their profound interest in the cause of Southern Independence.

When you are under privations and delays, and you become restive and you pant for inopportune conflict, its motto exhorts you to *patience* and represses the murmur on the lips.

When the order peals along the ranks to rush upon the perilous edge of battle, it exhorts you to *courage;* and when the wild surges of battle rage around you, it gives you the watch-word to mount and ride to *victory.*

I need not remind you that there is nothing so wins the gratitude and admiration of a people, as the brave soldier who battles for high achievement in his country's cause. Tennessee has a heroic fame as broad as civilization. Her gallant sons turned the tide of disaster at King's Mountain. Their impetuous valor carved its way to the southern gulf through the territory of the fierce and hostile Creeks; they covered their country with a blaze of renown on the plains of New Orleans. They mingled in the triumphal march through Mexico until the American cannon thundered its notes of victory above the crown of the Cordilleras. More than a hundred battlefields attest their valor. You, soldiers of the Eighth Regiment, are not expected to lower the standard of our former renown a hair's breadth; but we have confidence that you will fight up to it, and beyond it, if possible.

Religiously trusting in the God of battles, take this standard sheet, and beneath its folds chastise the insolence of the Northern vandals, who would invade our free and "Sunny South," devastate our fields, burn our houses and villages, dishonor our females, Africanize our civilization, proscribe our religion, subjugate our people, and overthrow our government.

Vindicate our rights and honor, and on your return mothers, wives, sisters, and all our female patriots will lavish their smiles and blessings upon you.

Jno. M. Bright.

At the conclusion of which the Adjutant handed the banner to Maj. W. H. Botts, who replied in substance as follows:

Fellow-Soldiers: The ladies of Lincoln county, through their commissioner, the Hon. John M. Bright, present to you this beautiful banner, with the request that you accept the same as a token of their especial sympathy and regard for you as soldiers, and as an expression of their profound interest in the cause of Southern independence. On your behalf I have been requested to receive this beautiful present, and to tender to the fair donors the profound gratitude and thanks of every member of this regiment for the same.

Beneath its folds the fair donors exhort you to chastise the insolence of the Northern vandals, who would invade our free and Sunny South, devastate our fields, burn our houses and villages, and debase and dishonor our females.

From the time we parted with our wives and mothers and sisters in Tennessee, and took up the line of march for the seat of war, wherever we have seen the face of a woman we have been exhorted to chastise this mighty and unnatural foe of ours. The waving of handkerchiefs, the clapping of their glad hands, the smiles that played across their beautiful faces, in every village and at every depot, as we dashed along on the iron horse, were unmistakable signs of the abiding interest they feel in the great cause in which we are enlisted.

Occasionally we have met up with men who have turned to us the cold shoulder, looking upon us with cold indifference, but not a single instance have we seen where woman has not shown a warm devotion to our cause, evincing a high regard for us. Yes, while the men have stood silently by, and looked with cold indifference upon the almost famishing and thirsty soldier, as he passed along his wearisome journey, the ladies (God bless them!), like ministering angels, have rushed to the door, and from thence to the fence, handing such refreshments as they could gather up in such haste to the thirsty and hungry soldier. Oh, what an exhortation! What an appeal to the warm hearted and brave Tennessean to fight, and, if need be, die, in defense of such a noble race of women. And now, fellow-soldiers, that we are almost in sight of the enemy's encampment, in hearing of his drums, here in the mountains of Pocahontas county, of Northwest Virginia, our women, fearing our patience might become threadbare and our courage weaken, remind us again of our homes, friends, and above all, of our patriotic women, and the deep interest they take in us and the great cause in which we are enlisted, by presenting to us this banner, inscribed, " Patience, Courage, Victory!" While from the great deep of our hearts we thank the ladies for the beautiful banner, we, if possible, thank them much more for the very appropriate motto inscribed thereon, and to ourselves, fellow-soldiers, let us pledge to our women everywhere, and more especially to those who sent us the banner, that we will obey their patriotic teaching in all things, and carry this banner in triumph, unstained and untarnished, patiently, yet courageously, through this war, to victory, and return with it to Tennessee, and, upon some suitable occasion, present it again to the ladies, and ask them to receive it back again in the same spirit in which it was presented. Our exhortation shall then be to them, that in some secure and lovely spot that banner shall be placed with their own hands where it may be preserved, from generation to generation, as a fit emblem of woman's devotion to free and liberal government.

While one of the chosen "Twelve," for a small compensation, betrayed the Son of God, another denied Him, and He was led up the rugged hill of Calvary by wicked men for crucifixion, and his Apostles followed at a great distance, we learn that many women were there, beholding afar off, which followed Jesus from Gallilee, administering unto him, and when he was taken from the cross and buried, the weeping Mary and other good women still lingered about the place for awhile, and were found next at the grave. The poet, in alluding to this sublime subject in connection with woman, truly said:

> "Not she with traitorous lips her Saviour stung;
> Not she denied Him with unholy tongue;
> She, while Apostles shrank, could danger brave—
> Last at His cross, earliest at His grave."

Thank God! let man be what he may in the nineteenth century, woman can justly boast that her sex has never taken the march backwards, but now boasts of a higher degree of refinement, intelligence and beauty than she could in any other age of the world; and yet the men of the North say of her that she is to be disgraced, dishonored, her proud spirit humbled, when the Southern soldier is conquered. We scorn his insolence and defy his power to do either. If he should be able to conquer in the field the Southern soldier, we are gratified to know that we have left behind us a band of courageous women, who will, when the enemy shall penetrate the interior of our country, and commence his work of devastation, welcome him with bloody hands to hospitable graves, and protect their own homes from disgrace and dishonor.

At the conclusion of the Major's address, the ensign and color guard came up in front of the speaker, viz.: G. W. Overstreet, ensign, and Corporals R. J. B. Gant, W. T. Woodruff, E. E. Cullom, R. F. Stegall, G. W. Tunstal, G. M. Ray, L. Croft and M. C. Cotton, who received the banner from the hands of the Major, who addressed them a few appropriate remarks. The color guard accepted the responsibility resting upon them, and said, each for himself, that *that* flag should go back to the fair donors unstained and unpolluted by the unhallowed touch of a live Yankee.

With that gallantry known to all Tennesseans, this flag was preserved for many days, and it passed through many contests of danger and blood, and it was never permitted to be furled in dishonor or disgrace. The thanks of the regiment were tendered to those good ladies, and we much regret that we cannot give the names of the ladies who sent it to us. Many of them, as well as many of the regiment, have passed away since that day to their peaceful homes, and in the bright memories of those of us who remain will be cherished happy recollections of this act of devotion and sympathy on the part of the good and noble women of Lincoln county.

The people of the South will long cherish fond recollections of the devotion of the women of the South. Though "white winged peace" has blessed the nation for more than twenty years, the government—"this glorious government"—continues to visit its vengeance upon the South. Until we are all treated in fact and in truth as one people, with equal rights and immunities, we fear there can be no peace. For this fear or apprehension we might assign various reasons and causes, though we would not for the "gold of Peru" detract from the fame of our country that almost obsolete distinction of the "best government the world ever saw."

Perhaps one fact will illustrate this idea. As you pass rapidly through the old battle ground of Stone's River, at Murfreesboro, Tenn., on some railroad train, enough will meet your eyes to sadden your heart. How beautifully and tenderly is the city of the Federal dead kept!

The Garden of Eden, with all its rich bowers of mellow fruits, perennial flowers and crystal waters, could be but a little better guarded. Each grave is marked with marble, and over the bones of gallant men nature's God spreads His carpet of green and gold. Man, with the money vaults of a powerful nation, stands there with all his power to perpetuate the beauties and defend from vandalism this sacred spot. And this is right in one sense. But the contrast! A short distance from this holy spot can be seen another garden of the dead, and how different does it appear!

Go, look at it—compare the two! A few old decaying boards stand as faltering signals of the greatest soldiers ever on the earth. The little wasting mounds are fast finding a common level with the surface. Vandalism is right on and among the graves of the heroic dead. The corn, the potatoes, the cabbage, flourish right at their heads and feet, and soon the soil that now covers the bones of those gallant and good men, will be made to give life and vigor to cotton, wheat or corn. No flowers here! no grapes waving there! no paved streets! no guarded walks found here! All is dead, above and below. The covetousness of man impatiently awaits the time when nature will level all that marks the place as the place of the dead, and with a demoniac yell he will drive over it his ploughshare and his reaper, and soon there will be no thought of the place.

Why this invidious distinction? In death there can be but one solemn destiny. Human agency, human wrong, human ambition and folly, are all swallowed up in death, and any individual, who, in this Christian age, would dare push his hatred and malice into the grave of a dead neighbor, would be spurned from society as a foul fiend and become a "hiss" and "by-word" for all honest people.

Will the comparison or analogy suit this glorious country? "This is the best government the world ever saw," some people say. What are those bones in the Confederate graveyards now doing, that they are to be despised and neglected by the government, while those of the Union soldiers are preserved and kept sacred and holy? and that too, at the expense of millions of dollars, all public money, belonging alike to the whole nation—North and South. No doubt, in that old decaying and neglected Confederate cemetery, there are the bleeching bones of some loved son, brother or father from every State in the South. To look out and witness the treatment and partiality shown by the government to those bones, is not well calculated to cause people to forget and forgive, or admire, to say nothing about love. The mean villainy of the politician manifests itself in the administration of the government; and until a grander and more elevated patriotism takes hold of and administers this government, we do not utter many hopeful prophecies.

We are aware that this may cause the official vagabonds and sap-suckers, to turn up their "pug" noses in contempt; but honest men know we speak an honest and solemn truth, when we say this thing is doing more to perpetuate enmity between the sections, and hatred towards the government, than any other act now known.

It is a national disgrace and shame. In life the fathers and mothers of the South loved their children, and in death, though on fields of battle, they will love and revere their graves, and never cease to curse the hand or power that desecrates them. The government throws its protecting power and care over the Union dead, and visits its spite and hatred on the poor harmless bones of the Confederate dead. For this, no excuse, founded in reason, can be given.

PART II.
BIG SPRINGS.

BIG SPRINGS.

On Monday, the 26th of August, considerable excitement existed in camps, caused by the report that the Federals had attacked our picket lines. To ascertain the truth of this, Capt. J. L. Bryant, of Company A, of the Eighth Tennessee Regiment, was directed to select two men from each company of the regiment, and make an examination of the country for the enemy. After being out for two days, he reported no enemy to be found.

On the 28th, our regiment was ordered to move on and still further up into the mountains, and after a slow march through torrents of rain, through mud and through branches of water, a distance of about eight miles, we were halted at Big Springs. This country was similar in its general features to that of Edray. It was almost impossible to get level ground enough on which to erect a tent or set a camp-kettle. Here we remained for several days, and nothing of any importance occurred, only an occasional report of the near approach of the "Yankees" kept up a little feeling among the men. It never failed to rain about every thirty minutes, and it fell in broken showers as a matter of convenience, but in large quantities.

On Sunday, Sept. 1, we were ordered to put our guns,

bayonets, cartridges and cartridge-boxes in perfect order, and for some time the whole regiment was busily engaged in this work. After some time thus spent, we were put on dress parade, and the line looked more like a compact row of Mexican mud huts than soldiers, and especially Tennesseans. Water was plentiful, but energy and soap were at a premium and scarce, or not fully appreciated.

At 10 o'clock a young man of fine abilities (Alex. McKenzie) preached to the regiment. He was a brilliant young minister, and belonged to the Cumberland Church. We are informed he died during the war, at some point not now remembered. He was brought up in Lincoln county, where he had many friends and relatives.

This closes our first Sunday at Big Springs.

Just across the little branch Col. Robt. Hatton's regiment was encamped, and among them we met some kind and valued friends, and here it was the Sixteenth Regiment, commanded by Col. John H. Savage, came up and joined us. Here began the work of these two regiments under Gen. Donelson, constituting what was known as Donelson's Brigade, consisting of about sixteen hundred men able for active duty.

We remained here for several days, doing considerable picket duty and living on very short and scattering rations. Indeed the roads were in such condition but little, if anything, could be gotten to us. We made use of all the blackberries and chickens we could find, and where a little patch of corn was found we generally got that too. Mud and water were the prevailing commodities in that section at that time.

At Big Springs we remained in comparative ease (except being pinched by hunger) until Monday, the 9th of September, when very suddenly orders came for us, about 2 o'clock P. M., to get ready to move out, with only one blanket to the man. our cartridge-boxes having been previously well filled.

THE MARCH OVER THE MOUNTAIN.

About 5 o'clock in the evening the Eighth and Sixteenth regiments moved out together. and up on a hill about three miles distant we halted, and without a single tent rested on what was called Valley mountain for the night. Something getting out of order with the clouds it did not rain on us that night, to the astonishment of all. While on this mountain a detail of two men from each company was made, who were supplied with axes, picks and spades or shovels, and ordered out in advance of the regiments to cut and make passways for the troops. This work was begun by daylight of the 10th, and they preceded us in our perilous passway by hacking on trees, removing in many instances impending rocks and huge bowlders on mountain sides. They cut steps down the sides of hills and mountains, and cut and bent down small trees whenever convenient to furnish something for the troops to hold to in ascending and descending the mountainous route selected for us. The Eighth regiment went in advance, and the Sixteenth closed up after us. This sappers and miners company was commanded by Captain Bryant, of company A, of the Eighth, and had a hard time of it on that day. We frequently halted and waited for some dangerous declivity to be so arranged that we could get either down or up it or over it, for we had purposely abandoned all roads and had to take our chances in the woods. We traveled on no such thing as a road, if indeed a road could exist in that country, which we doubt. Over mountains and down mountains and up mountains we silently moved on all that day, having strict orders to keep perfect silence during the whole march. We had a guide who went in front, who in appearance looked like he was just out of some dark cavern or hollow tree, and was a second cousin to the ground-squirrel family. He wore an old-fashioned bee-gum hat, and there was fully as much of the hat as there was of the guide, and each was about the same age, both relics of the Revolutionary war, and both moss covered. Around this old hat was tied a white rag, which could be seen through the dense timber and huge mountain cliffs, bobbing along like an old crippled ghost. He was always in front, and was the bell-wether of the flock. Shortly after 12 o'clock we began to descend one of the most rugged and dangerous looking mountains we ever saw. The abyss below was frightful, and the awful precipice seemed utterly to defy us. But go we must. Moving round and round, meandering from point to point, swinging to limbs, leaping from cliff to cliff, aiding each other by holding to each other's hands and forming a kind of chain made of strong arms and brave hearts, the men slowly and gradually descended. Once at the foot of the mountain, we remember quite vividly, we stood and gazed up the rugged heights we had descended, and thought our descent a most miraculous performance. The mountain was almost perpendicular, and huge cliffs or rock mountain ribs projected out in seeming defiance of all human power and effort. How the officers got their horses down the mountain may seem curious to many. It was said that the old guide, who was not of this age or country, and who possessed mysterious and bewitching powers, took the horses to pieces on top of the mountain and carried them down piece at a time, and when all were down, at his magical command each piece took its proper place, and then the animals stood again living beasts ready for duty, and perhaps this is about as good an explanation of the affair as we are now able to give, but we do not say that it is altogether correct, and leave the matter for others to explain.

As soon as the advance company reached the foot of the mountain, they began to ascend another, as there was but a small space of land between the two. In point of height and ruggedness, and seeming "impassibilities" rolled up in first-class mountain order, the adjacent one was almost equal to any we had seen. To those who were engaged in the work of climbing up this mountain what we here say will be readily recognized as strictly true.

Each man in the rank and file of the two regiments started out early that morning equipped as follows:

An old-fashioned percussion cap, smooth barrel army musket, weighing perhaps ten pounds, the old-fashioned cartridge box of those times filled with cartridges, attached thereto a bayonet and scabbard, all weighing about fifteen pounds; a blanket or quilt twisted up and tied around the shoulders and neck; a canteen filled with water, and an empty haversack, making in all about thirty pounds of baggage to each soldier. We were not only our own baggage wagons, but our own ordnance wagons, water carts and tent carriers, and all, save the commissary part. This part of the army train was conspicuously absent, and the absence much lamented.

Here perhaps we should state that at about 1 o'clock at night, and while yet on Valley mountain, and our advance out, orders came to the two regiments for a detail of three men from each company, to go off at some point, not now remembered, and cook two days' rations, and with orders to report back at 6 o'clock next morning with the rations. These cooks were promptly detailed and started off; but with many of us this was the last time we ever saw or heard of the rations on that march, for by some culpable mismanagement or carelessness the rations did not reach us; and having started out that morning with little or nothing to eat, the condition of our appetites can be imagined when we landed at the foot of the first mountain, and with orders to immediately ascend another. Some of the companies were fortunate enough to get their bread, and this was divided among us with true soldier-like liberality. This bread was composed of an inferior grade of flour, made up without salt, lard or "shortening" of any kind, and cold water alone used. To get a piece of this bread in any sort of shape for home consumption, we had to use a pick-axe on it or drive our bayonets through it and gradually work it into fragments so we could swallow it, for no man in the army could "chew" it. With this as our food, supplemented with a quantity of water and some sand thrown into our stomachs to assist and sharpen up our digestive machinery, our condition can be better imagined than properly described.

But up the next mountain we must go. Our pick and axe company, or sappers and miners, so called, were ahead of us digging steps into the huge mountain sides, making here and there pathways around some monster projecting rock or deep cut or frightful abyss, cutting and bending down small trees and sapplings, uniting them together in such manner as to form a sort of hand railing by which we could pull up by, gradually winding at times around on the edges and cliffs of precipices, when, if a step was made out of the exact line or path, we knew nothing would remain of us but a mangled body at the bottom in a moment's time, and thus we put in the remainder of the day in climbing up this mountain.

Our old guide was still on hand, and busy. Evidently he had been raised amid mountains—perhaps on mountain peaks—for the whole affair seemed to him a pleasant pastime.

Away in the distance, and far up or down some mountain side, he could often be seen up in a tree or standing on some elevated cliff, with his hat and white rag full in view of the advance guard. But again it may seem to many a problem how our field officers got their horses up such a place.

Here our old mysterious, mystical guide, whose surname was *Samuel*, comes to our relief again. It is said he caused a deep slumber to come over the horses, and he then took them apart and carried the pieces up, one at a time, and put them all in a heap, and when all up, at his command, " Horses come forth," each horse stood up again, a willing and obedient charger, and soon our two gallant colonels and other officers set on them ready for other duties. If this is not satisfactory, we confess we are not able to explain the matter any better, and commit the task to old man " Hobgoblin."

Just on the top of this mountain, and in a hay field, we camped for the night, men falling down, completely exhausted, on the ground and passing immediately into the wearied soldier's sleep. We had not a tent, not a camp kettle, not a spark of fire, and not a thing to eat, except a soldier could be found now and then with one of those things cooked or manufactured out of flour and cold water. The hay or grass in the little field had just been cut, and many of us piled it up for beds, and with our guns under us, we slept and rested with an ease and comfort not often allotted to man. Thus ended our first day's march.

Next morning, the 11th of September, by daylight, the two regiments were quietly aroused, and without a single thing to eat, we were soon into line and began to move out again, with orders to maintain the strictest silence, and to keep "closed up ranks." The fates were against us again, as usual. Promises were made that at some designated point our cooking men would meet us with our two days' ration, and then we would get something to eat. To add to our discomfort, it soon began to rain. We marched out in a northwestern direction, and down hills and up hills, across branches and small creeks, still avoiding all roads or anything like a road. Wet, hungry, muddy, on we marched without a murmur, expecting every few minutes to be halted to receive our rations; but still they came not.

Maintaining the greatest silence, we moved more like wild beasts hunting some unexpected prey, than like civilized Tennesseans. We avoided all houses, if there were any in that country, and hugged closely the mountain gorges and overshadowing cliffs and dismal corners. We

BIG SPRINGS.

moved slowly of necessity, and as we moved it rained. The mountain sides became so soft and saturated with water that it was almost impossible to ascend or descend them, and when we had to march on the sides to reach some designated point, the effort was truly trying and testing on the men loaded down with their guns, cartridge-boxes, blankets and trappings. Quietly we moved on that day until about 3 o'clock P. M., when we were halted on top of a high ridge, and after resting about thirty minutes, two companies of the Eighth, Capts. Bryant's and Hall's, were called out, and each assigned a certain route alongside the mountain, and were ordered to go down the same, observing perfect silence. Away down from us was a deep gorge or hollow, closely hemmed in by mountains on both sides. Here Capt. Bryant's company was assigned to the right, and Capt. Hall's to the left. There may have been other companies from the Sixteenth detailed, but we do not now remember them. However, with this arrangement, and the principal body of the brigade in the center, we began to advance down into a deep hollow below, and soon found a little branch, which we afterwards learned was Becca's Run. Creeping along these mountain sides as best they could, hidden by the low undergrowth and bushes, these two companies advanced in as rapid manner as possible. After being in motion about two hours, suddenly a gun fired some distance in advance of the main body of troops, and hastening up, we soon came in view of a little log cabin, and found in it three women and some children. Capt. Hall had, with his company, captured four living, and, to our sight, well dressed, fat looking "Yankees," so called. They were out as advance pickets, and had been surprised and captured. Without scalping these "huge monsters," as we then regarded them, they were placed under a guard, and were looked at with much curiosity, being the first of the kind we had ever seen. Indeed they were the first uniformed, living "Yankees" any of us had ever seen.

But a short time was spent here, and soon onward and down the branch, or run as it was called, we went for a distance of about one mile, when two more keen reports of muskets rang out in the mountain fastnesses, and here our men had captured two more prisoners, and fatally wounded two, who were trying to make their escape up the mountain on Capt. Bryant's side. Still pushing right on, the advance took a captain and two privates, quietly sitting on the creek bank fishing. So silently did these three companies proceed along the mountain, this squad was captured before they were thinking of our presence.

Here Col. Savage, who had been in command of the rear guard, was ordered by Gen. Donelson to the front, and he took command of the advance guard. Passing to the front, he found Capt. Bryant's and Capt. Hall's men nearly exhausted, and he ordered Capt. L. N. Savage's company of the Sixteenth Regiment to the front and in the center. This company was, perhaps, the best company in the brigade, not a man in it being over thirty-two years of age. Capt. Savage was mounted, and was by the side of Col. Savage in all the dashes he made that evening on different pickets. It is impossible to give in perfect detail all that took place on our march down this creek or run, for we are writing from a private's standpoint, and knowing nothing of war councils and plans only as developed in action.

The Federals, not expecting a "Johnny Reb" was within twenty miles of them, supposed the shooting above them was by their own men, and hence it aroused no suspicion at the time. Indeed, our advent was a complete surprise to them, and we had so far but little trouble. Still moving down the stream for another mile, we ran up on forty-three of them busily engaged in cooking. With Bryant's company on the right still crawling along under the bushes, and Hall's company on the left concealed by a thick undergrowth, they both got nearly in the rear of the house in which they had their quarters, and before they knew of our presence they found themselves completely surrounded. Just at this time Col. Savage, of the Sixteenth Regiment, came up to the front of the troops in the center, and in company with Col. Fulton and Capt. Al. Ewing and the advance guard, ordered the regiments to "double-quick" and charge on this picket force. With what many thought a reckless act, Savage ran his horse up to the yard gate, and made him jump over it and right into the midst of the Federal pickets. One of the pickets raised his gun to fire on him, but with drawn sword and in a clear, ringing voice, Col. Savage demanded their surrender, and they fired not a gun. We remember with a lively interest this incident of the bravery of the man. He seemed to be ever on the alert, and anxious for the "fray." To many of us he was a stranger, but there seemed to be about him something that at once attracted attention and admiration.

But here we must add, when the order came for the center to move up at "double-quick" time, every one thought that we were going right into a fight, and nearly every man threw away his blanket or quilt in order to have the free use of himself and his trusted old musket, and of all the general scattering of old blankets, coats and old quilts that men ever witnessed, the shucking off of such things took place here. And it must not be forgotten that it continued to *rain* during these performances. After this last capture, many of the boys who were in advance helped themselves to the good crackers and meat these troops were preparing for their supper, and it was divided out among the men, who by this time were almost famishing.

Something to eat at this stage was more highly prized than gold and silver, pearls and rubies, and how they kept from eating up those fat, saucy-looking "Yankees" we cannot now tell.

The prisoners were soon put into line and all searched, and some one found on the person of Sergeant McLane this letter from a young lady, and we submit it and shall let others comment on it. Suffice it to say that if the author of it is yet living she will no doubt be astonished somewhat should she ever find it here. Evidently she was a woman of intelligence, true courage and devotion:

Letter found on Sergeant McLane.

Wheeling, Va., Aug. 28, 1861.

Mr. W. B. McLane:

Sir—By the reception of your letter I perceive you are in the so-called Union army in Western Virginia, where I trust you may receive that which every invader of Virginia's soil deserves.

I would have you remember I am a Virginian, and if I were not, my sense of right, truth and justice must teach me ever to recoil from one who has so far forgotten his manhood—so far forgotten that he was made in the image of his God—that he will engage in committing the most horrible outrages, plundering, aye, murdering, for such every sensible person must regard the death of Gen. Garnet, of whom you speak.

Coward that you are, you know it was not done in an honorable way, even had it been in a just cause. And so you make a great ado about murdering the brave Garnet, whose life was worth the whole army of your hirelings. And the prisoners you speak of: there are a few pent up here in Camp Carlyle. I presume they are like those captured by your command of outlaws.

They are not soldiers, but private citizens, taken from their homes, their families. One, an old gray headed man, was taken from his cornfield where he was at work, and why? "O, because he was a secessionist." No, it was because he *dare* be a man and assert his rights; because, forsooth, he did not toss high in the air his cap and shout for the Union—union of white and black.

As to dressing in the clothes of the Confederates to deceive them, that would be in conformity with your former acts, which have been so *noble*, so *brave*, history does not furnish a parallel. No doubt, by such disguise you may be enabled to shoot a few more in the back whom you have not the courage to face. No, I presume I would not recognize you in the dress, for I doubt not but that I should gaze and wonder what manner of beast could have the presumption to don the attire of a *gentleman*.

From the contents and style of your letter, I judge you were not aware of my sentiments. This will enlighten you on that point; also, that all intercouse between us must cease from this time. P.

The prisoners were, as soon as possible, put under the keeping of Lieut. Bonner, of the Mulberry company (Capt. Thrash is commanding that company, having been elected when Capt. W. L. Moore was elected Lieutenant-Colonel to fill his place), and Lieut. W. C. Griswell, of Higgins' company, with a detail of twenty men.

But a few minutes were spent here, for just as soon as the men could be gotten together we were marched off up to the right, and over another mountain. In the perpetual rain that was now falling the climbing of the mountain was now nearly impossible. The men had, however, relieved themselves of their blankets, heavy coats and quilts, for no more attention was given them after they were first thrown aside, to rush forward and capture the squad of forty-three heretofore mentioned.

Almost exhausted, they continued to struggle and pull up by bushes, stumps and trees, until at last the top began to be reached, and on we dragged our way across and down what was called Hannah's Run (creeks are called runs out there), and here darkness began to close in on us.

On still we moved, and soon we were led up to the left and began to ascend another mountain, but turning a little to the right, we crossed a spur of the same. Col. Savage's regiment, it must be remembered, over all these paths and mountain routes, was in the rear of the Eighth, and how they managed to get along, following our slippery pathway and footsteps, we cannot tell. That they were men with iron constitutions and determined wills, no one can question. Those who know anything of army marching do not have to be reminded that to march in the rear of an advancing regiment increases the labor and fatigue almost twofold. Especially is this the case in traveling up and down mountains.

After our advance company had reached the top of this

spur of "Flood mountain," as the men afterwards called it, we were halted to give the remainder of the regiment and the Sixteenth time to get up and into close ranks.

It was by this time as dark as midnight blackness, and so complete was the darkness, and so solid, that many of the boys declared they could cut it up into pieces, and some, "they say," tried to eat it. But nothing daunted, and knowing not where we were going, we soon began to descend a little pig pathway as it seemed to us, feeling our way down as best we could. Wandering about over these mountains, seemingly without any point of destination and with no intelligent instructions to the men, the god of the rain cloud seemed to have been aroused from his hiding place, and lines soon began to break in the dark cloud banks and the light of the stars came peeping down upon us as if in pity, and just as our advanced company reached the foot of the mountain they discovered they were right on the outpost picket of a strong fortification, behind which stood over ten thousand Federal soldiers. A halt was made, and soon the word was passed back up the line that we had reached almost the jaws of certain death. Bryant with his company was in front, and being a cool, cautious man, full of discreet courage, he awaited orders.

Gen. Donelson, Cols. Fulton and Savage and our guide had by this time passed to the front, and were with the advance as we descended this mountain.

A brief consultation was here held, the guide insisting, as we understand, that we must push on and into the camps of the enemy that night.

Cols. Savage and Fulton, with a cool, deliberate judgment, protested and urged that something had gone wrong; that a mistake had occurred somewhere, and that such an attack, with men in the condition we were in, was folly and nonsense.

In a short time the word was quietly passed along the line to "about face" and move out.

We do not pretend to say who caused that blunder, but we do say that it now seems to us our escape from a general massacre was miraculous. Exhausted and famishing, many of us barefooted, there we stood in a huddle, encompassed by mountains, an easy prey for the enemy. To add to all this, we are of opinion that not a gun could have been fired, for the guns and loads were also drenched in rain and water. Slowly, and with drooping and despondent feelings, exhausted and almost famishing with hunger, we turned and marched back again, and before we could reach the top those friendly stars had been hidden again by dark embankments of clouds, across which a flash of lightning would occasionally glare.

Once back on this mountain, and the rain descending in perfect torrents, without shelter and in utter confusion, the two regiments fell down in their own chosen style, and such a night as we spent there was never passed through by any men before. True to the instincts of his nature, we remember that Col. Fulton, feeling so anxious for the return of his advance men, stood at the top of the mountain as they came up and assisted them in getting up safely to the top. By this time eternal darkness seemed fastened upon that mountain. The windows of the heavens were wide open, and rain in torrents fell as it never fell before since the flood.

Without a single ration or food of any kind, without a blanket or tent, and with nothing but our arms, we spent one of the most terrible nights ever spent or passed through by men in any country or any age.

The black darkness around and about us, the skies and the stars hid from us, the howling mountain winds rushing over us, the flood clouds pouring out their contents upon us, down on the ground the men fell almost as fast as they reached the top, and taking the sides of trees, stumps, logs and rocks for shelter, there they remained during the night. Occasionally some one would call out for "more water," as it would wash under his sleeping apartment.

The prisoners who had been captured during the day were placed by order of Gen. Donelson under the immediate charge of Lieut. William Bonner, who of necessity had to remain on duty and wide awake.

About midnight a bear got among the men, and soon the alarm was raised that a wild bear was in our ranks. It created some excitement, and during the excitement the prisoners attempted to escape, but they failed. All the bears and wolves in those vast mountains would not have created much fear that night with the troops, for many began to feel like "yielding up the ghost," or were becoming desperate. At best the soldier's camp is not the safest place for bears, even under favorable circumstances. Rain fell incessantly all night. But little resting or sleeping was done by any one. At last "old gray morn" came peeping slowly over the east hills, and just as soon as it was light enough for the men to see, they began to work on their guns and to draw out the loads, for not a single gun in the brigade would fire. Of all the picking, hammering, rattling of ramrods, rubbing, twisting out bullets and wet powder from old muskets ever witnessed, perhaps the occasion here presented was never surpassed. The wet loads had to be drawn from the guns and the guns thoroughly dried before they could be reloaded. To do this much noise and confusion existed. The popping of caps, the shooting of blank cartridges, intermingled with the Babel-like confusion existing at the time, all contributed to a general "hoodlum" on the mountain "that morning." If the brigade had been attacked that morning early, every man in it would have been captured or forced into immediate surrender. Not only were the charges or loads in the guns wet and could not be discharged, but nearly every cartridge-box and every cartridge were in the same condition. A more powerless or harmless brigade of troops could not have been found, and then we were in sight of ten thousand Federal troops, and could have been captured at one time without the firing of a gun.

Such a predicament, brought about by such culpable ignorance or want of efficiency, deserves the severest condemnation to this day. But thoughtful men are generally equal to emergencies, and especially was this the case here. The old wet loads were soon extracted by the men, their guns dried as fast as possible by resorting to every available means at hand, and just as soon as it was safe and proper to reload these old muskets were again reloaded with dry powder and buck-and-ball cartridges. The men needed no orders that morning; they did not await any. Every man seemed to realize the critical situation, and the fatigues and hardships of the two previous days and nights were for a time forgotten.

It was fully 9 o'clock in the morning before a single move was made, as it seemed we were to be kept there awaiting orders.

All at once a sharp report of several guns sounded at the foot of the mountain, and the voice of Col. Savage could be distinctly heard calling his men into line.

Col. Fulton ordered his men into line, and in forming many of the boys discovered for the first time that Gen. Lee had made his way to us, and was there with us. This was the first sight any of us ever had of him.

He looked like a hero. As he sat on his fine large white horse, half hid in the bushes, the greatness of the man could be easily distinguished, even by the casual observer, and alike by the common soldier in the *ruff*. Grand and dignified he sat there, the soldier and the Christian, a hero and a statesman, seeming to grasp the situation and to hold it in the hollow of his hand.

By the time the Eighth regiment had formed into line and reached within a short distance of the foot of the mountain, Col. Savage's regiment had engaged a picket force of about one hundred men, Federals who had slipped up in our rear. Soon the yell was raised, and as Savage's men began to advance the firing increased. The Eighth set up a big yell, and, with fixed bayonets, rushed down the side of the mountain towards the firing, but before they reached the point the Federal picket force made a disorderly and precipitate retreat. The Eighth soon reached the valley below, and forming on the left of Savage's regiment, orders were given for us to move out in double-quick time. Gen. Lee and his staff officers passed on near the front of the brigade. After we got into motion Gen. Lee and his staff rode up a piece on the mountain side, and with their spy-glasses reconnoitered the situation. Col. Savage's regiment was put in front this day. Hall's company of the Eighth was detailed as rear guard, and after moving off up a small creek called Hannah's Run, which, however, was much swollen that morning by heavy rains, they were placed in ambush on the side of the mountain, as it was discovered the Federal pickets were following us.

Gen. Lee and his aids here passed to the front. The brigade, moving rapidly for about one mile, halted, and soon shots were heard in our rear. The Federal pickets had pursued beyond the point where Hall's company was concealed in ambush. About seventeen of them were captured. These Federal pickets had also a guide, and as we are informed, this guide was wounded in the skirmishing that morning, and it is said our guide, on hearing this, went to the rear and found him sitting on a log, with his legs broken, and rushing upon him ran a bayonet through him and left him dead. Old Dr. Butcher, the name of our guide, then became somewhat famous with the boys.

It was reported that seven or eight of the Federal pickets were killed on that morning, but we do not know that this is true. Col. Savage lost one man killed early in the morning and one was wounded. Immediately after the capture of these last men, orders came for us to get out of that place in double-quick time.

Mountains, high and lofty, were on all sides of us, and we had to travel up a narrow valley, if it could be called such, which was covered by swollen streams from one side of one mountain to the other. Hugged in by the mountain fastnesses, orders for us to double quick came, and now one of the hard days fell on us. We moved in all the fancy gaits of a soldier—sometimes in a trot, sometimes in a run and sometimes in a walk, and many, by this time, going in a limp, and some on one foot. We did not halt for the water, but waded through, and often it reached our armpits.

It is no exaggeration to say that, in this march, and crossing the streams as often as we did, at least one half of the brigade lost their shoes and had to travel barefooted. On and on we went, winding around and around, and following up the stream until about 4 o'clock in the evening we began to ascend a small rounded back mountain, and at last when the rear guard was slowly coming up, orders were given us to rest; but there was no rest for us. All this time, it must be remembered, we had had nothing to eat. Gen. Lee, it should here be stated, rode back to the rear and awaited the coming up of the rear guard, who then had the prisoners captured by them. He seemed anxious and solicitous for us.

He remained with us during that day, sometimes in the rear and sometimes in the front, and often up and down the line, but not a word did he utter to the men, that we remember.

But again, on top of the mountain, and riding up near the center of the brigade as the men lay scattered in utter confusion and exhaustion, some one raised a yell, and soon every man caught up the inspiration, and for a few moments the tops of the mountains around resounded with the shouts of men in honor of their great General, for by this time it had become known that Gen. Lee, learning of our critical situation on the night previous, had ridden all night to get to us and lead us out of the jaws of death, if possible; and when he thus rode up among the troops, is it any wonder that they hailed him as a deliverer? Yes, shout after shout rang out on the mountain wilderness, and with a grand and noble heart, he lifted his hat, and with a smile on his face, and bowing to the men on the left and on the right, he rode off and by many of us was never seen again.

In a few minutes a herd of fine looking cattle was discried near by, browsing on the mountain top. Starvation, like necessity, knows no law, and "bang" went a musket, and down came a fine fat bullock. This was only a signal for others, and it was bang, bang, until the entire herd lay at the mercy of a desperate and hungry army.

Little camp-fires soon sprang up, and as soon as a hide would be stripped off, a piece of the meat was cut out, and, without salt or bread, little sticks were procured, and when these could not be had, ramrods were used, and the meat was hung in the blaze and cooked or scorched, and no men ever ate sweeter meat. This was our only diet. The men killed, cut and ate just as much as they wanted, and many provided themselves with a mess or two for future emergencies. Beef alone, without bread or salt— good beef, cooked as this was that night, and under the conditions of our appetites, was relished as no king or potentate ever relished his most sumptuous banquets or feasts. This mountain was called Beef Mountain, and will never be forgotten by any one who participated in those events. To any member of the two regiments it is known to this day as "Beef Mountain," or "Jubilee Mountain," for here the shouts of the "delivered" were raised to the hero and the God of battles. But all is not told yet. Men who were now barefooted, pulled down almost to the earth with fatigue, and with no possible chance for anything better, took the raw hides from off the cattle, and made, as best they could, substitutes for shoes. Here we remained until next morning, without a tent or blanket, and with nothing in the way of comforts but our old muskets and green beef. We slept soundly, however, some on beds made of fence rails, others on piles of green leaves, and some, we suppose, roosted in trees and in fence corners. At any rate, the night passed over us, and next morning many were sent back to former camps. Early in the morning we were ordered into line, and began a rambling march over the tops of some small hills, as though we had been sent out snake hunting. Soon, to our surprise, we were going down that same "Becca's Run" we had passed down before, and winding around and around, taking "nigh" cuts and through woods and around huge bowlders, we came to the little cabin where we captured our first prisoners the day before. In this lonely hut the two women and some little white-headed children were found again, and the wounded Federal pickets, who had been shot the day before, apparently in their care. These women were attentive to them and did all they could for them, and no doubt with true womanly sympathy and courage. On we went, meandering from place to place, hunting for a fight, but no enemy could be found that day. Down still we moved, until we reached the house where the squad of forty-three prisoners had been captured two days before, and there, night closing in on us, we were marched up and on the side of the mountain on our left, and without a blanket, tent or fire, we rested, or attempted to do so, until morning. The declivity of the mountain was so great that we could lie in no other position than with heads up-hill and feet down-hill. Men took foothold against rocks, or astraddle trees or bushes, and some dug little holes in the mountain side and planted their feet in them, that they might not roll to the bottom. However, many of the men, after falling to sleep, lost their props or "scotches," and found themselves next morning some distance from where they laid down. A most uncomfortable night was spent here.

The line of the brigade, instead of being closed up and in order, was scattered over about three hundred yards of mountain side, and humanity never presented, perhaps, a more ghastly, if not ghostly, appearance than did our men the next morning. On we went the next day, moving from place to place, and crossing the spur of a mountain, we landed again on Hannah's Run, but at a higher point up the creek, and marching up this same stream we had traveled the day before, and thought it such a perilous way out of an almost certain slaughter-pen.

Our movement was indeed slow and in some disorder. Many began to give down under the long, constant strain, for the excitement was cooling down. The talk was fast becoming frightful and alarming. The old cow-skin shoes began to give out. Others were fast becoming barefooted, and the course of the march was plainly marked by the blood from the feet of the men. We had often heard of this character of terrible hardship among troops, but here it was before us in reality. Half naked, almost exhausted, faint, weary and sick, feet torn and lacerated and bleeding, the men slowly wended their way on and on, until at last we landed back on top of "Beef mountain," the very point we had left on the morning before.

In this terrible march we found no enemy but the wounded men at the cabin, and so far as we could see it was a day spent in fruitless toil and pain for no purpose. Resting for a short time on the top of this mountain, we were ordered down and off in a southern direction, and soon we found ourselves winding along another stream, called Mary's run. On we went, crossing and recrossing the stream, each time wading it, until near night, when news reached us that the enemy was in sight and on our right. Col. Savage was in front with his regiment, and Col. Fulton had some difficulty in getting his men well up and into line. Some stubbornness was manifested by some of his men, and some disobeyed his order, when all at once he, in unmistakable language, and drawing his sword, told the little squad he would cut the first man's head off who refused to obey his order. He soon discovered that one of the men could not walk. He got off his horse, put the man on him and fell into the ranks himself. Through all this march no kinder or more humane act was witnessed than this.

No enemy made their appearance, and no attack was made. On we marched, and dark overtaking us just as we reached what was called the "Big Road," leading from nowhere and going to the same place, we suppose, we were ordered up into a field on our left and along a fence to rest for the night.

Just as we got properly stretched out for a night's rest, orders came to get up and get out of that place.

Once again in motion, and turning up the "big road," we set out in an eastern direction. News reached us that a large force of Federal troops were just behind us, and the order came to "double-quick," but it had no effect, for the men moved slowly indeed. By this time it began to rain again and rained all night. At about 11 o'clock that night we were halted. The men began to build up large fires, made principally of fence rails, and finding some fields of corn near by, and a little cabbage patch, they roasted corn and eat raw cabbage for supper, and thought them special delicacies. In the mud, rain and water we spent again a most trying night. No language or pen can describe or paint the appearance of our brigade next morning. Humanity never presented its ragged edges more prominently. Anything but good humor was now boiling up to the surface among the men. They could not understand or appreciate all this suffering, and all this eternal push and strain, and no good resulting from it. Early that morning it was the general talk in camps that the whole affair was a failure, in consequence of Gen. Loring failing to perform the work assigned to him and his men. That he failed to do what he was instructed to do and was expected to do, there is no doubt. His excuse was that the rain and high waters prevented and made his part of the programme impossible to be carried out. This kind of excuse failed to allay the feelings existing in our ranks.

We were ordered into line and instructed to move out and up the road. We soon passed Gen. Loring's headquarters, so called, and as the advance of the brigade reached his quarters he "popped" upon a stump and stood as erect as a cock partridge in August, and gave the passing soldiers a grand military review. He wore a black suit of corduroy goods, with a broad-brimmed hat set on the side of his head, topped off with a flaming feather or cockade plume. Our men had been instructed to salute the General as they passed, but if a single man in the ranks did any such thing we did not see or hear of it. We heard several of the boys say if they could meet him in the woods they would take pleasure in giving him a few lessons in the manual of "shoot arms," or something to that effect. Not a voice was raised nor an old cap or hat lifted as we sullenly passed by. We all thought that if the rain and mud were not in our way, he could have no excuse. We had climbed up and down mountain after mountain, bared our heads to the rain and the storm, without shelter and but little raiment, and their excuse to us was a very poor one, and aroused nothing but contempt. But who was at the bottom fault we know not, and presume it now makes but little or no difference. One thing is certain, that our men and the officers of our brigade were not to blame, for we feel assured that our part was as faithfully done as men could do it. All our officers were vigilant, and endured and partook of every hardship that fell to their men, and are kindly remembered by those who passed through this ordeal.

Passing Loring's quarters, we continued to drag our weary selves along through mud and over hills and rocks, many with feet swollen and blood oozing out at every step, we rested at last, in the evening, at the point from whence we had started, "Valley Mountain." Here but a short halt was made, and with three miles yet to our camps at

"Big Springs," the men scattered and went in gaits to suit themselves. Some got back much earlier than others. In fact some of the boys did not get in until next morning.

Thus ended eight days, which, taken all together, was one of the most arduous and trying marches, we dare say without egotism, made by any troops during the entire war. We had captured about seventy prisoners and killed perhaps ten or more of the Federal troops. Many things recorded may seem incredible and many of no importance, and much of it a mere school-boy recitation; but those who participated in the march will bear witness that the tale is but too feebly told, and the scenes and hardships attending the campaign given without the coloring of a vivid imagination.

We pass rapidly by the sickness, the languor and disease that came afterwards. Many died whose names we do not remember. The prisoners, who were kept under guard by Lieut. Bonner and Lieut. Griswell, were sent off to Richmond under their charge. The name of the Yankee captain captured was Bruce, from Cincinnati, Ohio. He was highly spoken of by the officers who had him in charge as a perfect gentleman. There were also one civil engineer, two lieutenants and three sergeants in the list of prisoners taken on the march.

After our return to "Big Springs," our camping ground, several letters were written home, giving brief accounts of the campaign or march. We here insert the following one, written by Capt. Higgins to the Fayetteville *Observer*, which will be read with some interest:

HIGGINS' LETTER.

* * * To give you a minute detail of all that occurred on that day, or the seven consecutive days, would take more time and paper than I have to spare. Permit me to say, however, that Napoleon's trip across the Alps must sink into insignificance when the faithful historian describes the trip that Gen. Donelson's brigade made across the Alleghanies.

Napoleon's men looked upon him with reverential awe, with a degree of confidence never equalled; besides, they were clothed and fed, and had all the stimulating drinks the vineyards of France afforded, pressing forward in the hope of glory and of wealth; while we, unacquainted with the militarys kill of our general, knowing he had no experience; without food, and our bare feet making crimson the rough pebbles over which they trod, clinging now to some shrub till we could secure our footing in some crevice below, which if you missed, would tumble you headlong down unless some huge rock or tree should present an obstacle sufficient to check the double quick step movement; or, 'scaping this, would fall from rock to rock till you would be but a disfigured corpse, or living, a mangled object of pity; with no hope of reward save to free our country from the Goths and Vandals. Yet with a determination rarely equalled, never surpassed, pushing forward without a murmur, till the madly rushing stream below cooled our parching tongues, then casting our eyes heavenward (for the steepness of the mountain so directed them), we commence our slow and wearisome march upward, upward, until nature's self refuses longer to perform her functions, and we sink down into forgetfulness. Thus we traveled on the first day without being relieved by the sight of the enemy.

Resting as best we could, without fire, with unsalted beef for rations, without bread; with no covering but the lowering clouds, which, ever and anon, let loose upon our devoted heads their torrents of water, we slept as only exhausted men can sleep.

At daylight next morning we lifted our weary limbs from mother earth and again struck out across the mountains. I will not give you the names of the different peaks over which we passed. They are all spurs of the Alleghanies. We were now in the enemy's country, and had to keep a sharp lookout to prevent a surprise. At 12 M., the advance guard discovered the enemy's pickets. We were ordered to flank them, which we could only do by a double quick movement up the side of the mountain. It had been raining all day, and it was not only the most tiresome trip I ever underwent, but it was with the greatest difficulty we could keep our feet. Our Colonel, than whom there is not a braver or more magnanimous man in the army, abandoned his horse, led the way, and rushing upon them (there were four), ordered them to surrender or die. They surrendered without hesitation. They had first-rate muskets and minnie ball cartridges. The men were fine looking fellows, and did not seem dissatisfied with their position as prisoners. This was our first bloodless victory. We again pushed forward, went about half a mile, when we again came upon four more of their pickets, who were not so ready to surrender as the first. Two of them broke at full speed down the valley, but a shot from a musket in the hands of one of our men and a ball from the rifle of our guide brought them down. They paid dearly for their folly. The others surrendered.

Again we advanced, and again came upon their pickets, taking them prisoners, securing their guns, etc. We finally came upon the whole company from the Sixth Ohio regiment, who were quartered in a house from which they had driven the family. We took them completely by surprise and they surrendered without firing a gun. Two of the company were up on the side of the mountain, and ran at the top of their speed, but a couple of shots brought them to; they could not escape the unerring aim of our boys. We got some fine swords, guns, etc. The captain (Bruce) had a beautiful sword, a present from the citizens of Cincinnati, for his "noble efforts in defense of his country." He was a very intelligent man; said his company was sworn in for three years, but that the war was an unnatural one and could not last long.

We hid their guns securely, for we could not carry them, and formed again into line. The Orderly Sergeant of the captured company, by request, formed his company into line. We now left the little creek (Stewart's), and took a blind path across the mountain to take our position in the rear of the enemy's fortifications. We had killed four of the enemy and captured fifty, without the loss of a man, and felt proud of our day's work. We had yet three miles to travel to reach our destination. The rain began to descend in torrents, and it was nearly night. We reached it at last, nearly exhausted. We could see from the mountain the tents and camp fires of the enemy in the valley below. I and many others supposed the object was to surround them (we did not then know it was their strongest fortification), surprise and rout them, and take possession of their comfortable tents, provisions, etc., both of which were desirable objects, as we had not eaten anything scarcely for forty-eight hours, and there was a cool, chilling rain falling. We were badly mistaken, however. After marching down the hollow in the direction of their camps we halted. Our guide discovered that we were within gunshot of the most strongly fortified place in West Virginia, which was guarded by from 5,000 to 10,000 choice troops. This fact being reported to Gen. Donelson, he ordered us to ascend the mountain as noiselessly as possible. We could have been surrounded, cut off, butchered or made prisoners of (you should bear in mind that we only had about 1,300 men, and all our guns wet) by an alert enemy; but Providence again interposed in our behalf by sending torrents of rain, making night hideous by the howling winds and as black as Erebus. We gained the top without causing any alarm. Here we spent the night more disagreeably than I can describe. Let the curtain fall till morning.

At daylight next morning we were ordered to fall back several miles. Gen. Lee came to us in person, and informed us that the other commands had failed to come to time, and we must fight our way out. We started, left in front (Col. Savage's regiment was the left wing), but before proceeding fifty yards they were fired on by about one hundred of the enemy, killing one man and wounding one, both of Col. Savage's regiment. The fire was returned, and for a few moments the rattle of musketry was most musical to the ears of a soldier. Our regiment struck off at full speed, throwing aside blankets, haversacks, in fact everything but guns and cartridge-boxes, believing the fight had commenced, and fearing Col. Savage's regiment would be overpowered before we could reach them. They were entirely hid from our view. I flatter myself there never was more cool determination, more eagerness for the conflict, than that manifested by all the troops on that occasion.

Our Commissary, Capt. Ewing, on horseback, rushed ahead of the regiment and was in the thickest of the fight. Col. Savage ordered his men to charge. They raised a yell, which was answered by our regiment, now getting nearly upon them, and, fixing bayonets, rushed at them. The Yanks could not stand this, but fled in every direction. Eighteen ran into our lines and were captured. Thirteen were killed.

It was on Tuesday, the 17th of September, that we got back to Big Springs. Here we remained for a few days, eating gradually what little we could get, and washing our clothing, such as we had, and recuperating generally as best we could. On the 2nd we were ordered to cook four days' rations, which we proceeded to do. We had nothing at that time to cook but flour and fresh beef, and that of the most inferior quality. We had no salt, no lard, and the quality of the rations can be fully appreciated. Our ranks were greatly reduced by sickness and death, and the outlook was indeed growing quite gloomy. Yet it is right to say our officers did all they could for us. The mountain roads had by this time gotten in such a condition that it was almost impossible to get anything to us.

On Sunday morning, the 22nd, we folded our tents and silently and gladly bid farewell to Big Springs, in Pocahontas county, in West Virginia. That night we camped at the foot of Rich mountain.

On Monday, the 23d, we landed back at Marlin Bottom, on the Greenbrier river. Our sick had been left at Camp Edray, and much difficulty was overcome in removing them, but as fast as it could be done, they were transferred to Huntersville, a reference to which has been already given. While camped at Marlin Bottom, on the night of the 27th, there came another flood of rain, known only to that region of country, and such as no other country but that could produce. The water rose rapidly and was soon rushing in among our tents and under our beds of straw and leaves. Many had to move their tents on a hill side near by; and indeed everything was swept away that lay near the river bank but the celebrated "Jim Morton log," as the boys called it. The current and lashing waves, in their wild and mad rush, moved all before them, save this one *gigantic* piece, and there it remained up to the hour we left, as a fallen pyramid to mark the one place of our camp in the mountains.

On Sunday, the 29th, we moved out of the bottom and stopped one mile further on towards Huntersville. Here we remained for several days, nothing occurring of any interest. However, it should be mentioned that the Georgia regiment, under the command of Col. Blomley, which had been assigned to Donelson's brigade, did not march with us in our campaign over the mountains; and here, at Marlin Bottom, many of them died. Men never died more rapidly, it seemed to us, than did these Georgians in Northwest Virginia. One-half of that regiment, no doubt, died while we were in those mountains.

On Saturday, the 5th of October, we received orders to move out, and we did locate at new quarters. We took up our camps about one mile northeast of Huntersville. Here we struck a section of country that had not been invaded by any troops before, and for a while we had good living. Our camp equipage was remodeled, our appetites in a great measure satisfied, and the men began to *rebuild* themselves in all respects. The boys were learning to become successful forage masters. Here for several days we had an easy time. It was no uncommon thing to see some of the boys come into camps with a sheep or a bee-stand, an armful of cabbage (all bought and paid for, of course.)

The familiarity that soon grew up between the troops and many of the citizens was at times alarming in some respects. The widow at the little mill, and the "Crow" family were very kind, and will be remembered by many of us for many days. Here some fortifications were thrown up for practice and exercise, and in the main we had a good time generally.

While here, our friends at home, having learned something of our hardships and sufferings, through their benevolent societies and organizations, sent to the Eighth Tennessee Regiment a number of boxes filled with the most substantial and delicate provisions, just such as Tennessee wives and mothers know how to get up. On the receipt of this great blessing, as it was to us, Col. Fulton wrote the following letter back home, which speaks for itself:

HUNTERSVILLE, VA., Sept. 25th, 1861.

Mrs. Ross, President of the Ladies' Soldiers' Aid Society, Lincoln county, Tennessee:

I this day received, through your obliging Secretary, a very complimentary note, begging my acceptance of hospital stores for my regiment, with list of articles enclosed. With feelings, no language at my command can express, I accept for and in behalf of the Eighth Tennessee Volunteers the box of stores for their use so kindly tendered by your benevolent and humane Society, and earnestly beg you will accept for your Society the most grateful acknowledgements and heartfelt thanks of my command for the same.

Though we may march o'er hill and mountain plain, barefooted and on half rations; though we may expose ourselves by day and by night to all the vicissitudes of a life in camp and on the field; and though we may meet the enemy in a hand to hand to fight, contend for victory at the cannon's mouth; yet I much doubt if we exhibit so much devotion to our country or our country's cause, in defense of whose honor we have volunteered our services, as have the patriotic ladies of the South, and especially the ladies of the Soldiers' Aid Society of Lincoln county, Tennessee.

The minions of "Old Abe," the "Vandals" of the North, may boast their ability to subjugate the South, lay waste our homes, desolate our firesides, and march in triumph over our goodly land, but they never can accomplish their nefarious and unholy designs against a people whose fathers', husbands', sons' and brothers' hearts are strengthened and encouraged, and whose arms are nerved to battle by the sympathy and approbation, as well as the patriotic and self-sacrificing devotion of wives, mothers and sisters.

Permit me again to thank you for the honor and material aid rendered my regiment; and please accept for your Society the best wishes and prayers of the Eighth Regiment of Tennessee Volunteers. May your Christian mission receive its just reward, both in this and the life to come. Respectfully,

ALF. S. FULTON,
Col. Commanding Eighth Regiment Tenn. Vol's.

On Sunday, the 20th, our chaplain, David Tucker, preached to a large audience composed of members of the brigade, and had good attention.

Here many changes were made in the companies and regiments. Dr. Hall, Captain of company B, Eighth regiment, was promoted to chief surgeon of the Eighth regiment, and Dr. Gray, of Carthage, Smith county, Tenn., was promoted to brigade surgeon. Lieut. B. E. Malear, of company B, was promoted to captain of the same.

By this time the weather began to get cold, and we felt the necessity of winter clothing upon us.

Here we remained to the morning of the 10th of October, when we struck our tents, packed our baggage wagons, and made off for Lewisburg, Va. It rained on us every day we were making that march, the weather gradually getting colder. On the 13th we passed through Frankford, and rested that night within two miles of Lewisburg. The next day we passed on to Lewisburg, and camped that night five miles southeast of that place. Here we remained for several days. On the 16th a heavy snow fell and remained on the ground all day. On the 17th, and at this point, the Eighth regiment received the clothing that had been sent to them from their friends and relatives in Tennessee. To say we were glad and much rejoiced is giving a feeble expression to the feelings of the men on that occasion. The people at this place treated us very kindly. Indeed, the hospitality shown us was the first thing of the kind we had been favored with since our departure from Charlottesville.

We camped on the farm of a Mr. Robinson, and his daughter, a nice, intelligent young lady, devoted much attention to our sick men. She visited the camp frequently, bringing with her such things to eat as a poor, sick soldier can properly appreciate. Her kindness will never be forgotten by some of us. The McClure and Erwin families were also very kind, and gave many of the men who were unwell food and shelter.

At Trinity church, near by, a protracted meeting was going on, and many of the boys attended regularly, and, like "Burrel's" boarders, were always ready to receive an invitation to go and take dinner or remain all night, and they made it a rule never to refuse, and always remained as long as patience endured.

But these pleasures were necessarily of short duration. On Friday morning, about 9 o'clock, we struck tents, loaded our wagons and started for the Salt Sulphur Springs. As usual rain was falling, and this soon turned to sleet and ice. Traveling about ten miles that day we halted at Nelson's Grove. The next morning, Saturday, the 30th day of November, it was snowing, and we moved out slowly and passed on by Salt Sulphur Springs and other places not necessary now to mention here. On the 2d of December we landed at Red Sulphur Springs, and left on the third and camped that night at Hobbs' Ferry. On the next night we camped at Parishburg, and at Dublin the next. On Sunday, the 8th of December, and at this point, we received orders to go to Charleston, S. C., whither we went, traveling through North Carolina and Georgia before reaching Charleston. On Sunday, the 15th of December, 1861, we landed in that place, after having traveled by railroad a distance of about six hundred miles.

In this brief and very imperfect sketch of the campaign made by the Eighth and Sixteenth Regiments, we are aware many interesting incidents have been overlooked and many forgotten. We have of necessity been forced to rely in a great measure upon the memory of the living, taking an intermediate course of the various recollections as detailed to us. To Mr. N. O. Wallace, editor and proprietor of the Fayetteville *Observer*, and to Capt. James McAfee and Capt. Geo. W. Higgins, of the Eighth Regiment, we are indebted for many favors, as from them we have been enabled to extract and put together quite all leading facts here detailed. We might follow these two regiments up to the close of the war, but such was not our design or purpose, and that task is now in abler and more competent hands. No two regiments in the Southern army ever passed through more trying ordeals and suffered more than did the Eighth and Sixteenth Regiments of Tennessee Volunteers, though passing under many different and gallant and chivalrous commanders.

We lay no claim to perfect accuracy, and in our effort we have studiously avoided the use of fancy's paintbrush, or the delicate and refined pencil work of imagination. We much regret we have not been able to give in detail more about the men and the doings of the Sixteenth Regiment, but our sources of information have been very meagre, and besides, our effort in that direction has been much embarrassed by another, who has, we learn, a complete work "copyrighted," and in that, no doubt, those gallant men will receive, as they richly deserve, all proper and becoming commendation and praise for their long suffering, endurance and fidelity.

CONCLUSION.

We beg to say, in conclusion, that at this day and time, the scenes here detailed may appear as a mere speck or trifle in the great mass of events of the late war, and fill but a small space in the grand picture so beautifully drawn out by others, but if we go back twenty years, not only in our own land, but in all the nations of Europe, mankind never made as rapid improvements in the science of war (if it be a science), as within the last twenty-five years. The people of this continent were essentially a people of peaceful pursuits, and more especially in the South, "but having their guns and their trees and their freedom," no power on earth could ever conquer them. No man knows anything of his power of endurance until tested, as this campaign over Cheat Mountain—the Alps of America—on whose rugged edges and cliffs the blood of many Tennesseans was left in their weary tracks, fully proves.

We submit our little effort to our friends, and ask them to let fall over it a broad mantle of charity. No doubt some will be of opinion that many things embraced within these pages, and much of the matter, ought to have been left out; but our purpose has been to give a faithful statement of public sentiment in this country in 1861, as well as the facts in relation to the campaign of the Eighth and Sixteenth Regiments over Cheat Mountain. We hope what we have done and said will hurt no one; if it does, let it hurt.

The object sought and the purpose to be subserved is one of a mere local and individual interest, and no fame or fortune is sought or expected. The entire labor has been bestowed at the instance and request of a few friends, and much of it has been a " work of love" to us.

PART III.

BRIEF BIOGRAPHICAL SKETCH
—OF—
ALFRED S. FULTON,
COLONEL EIGHTH TENNESSEE REGIMENT.

COL. ALFRED S. FULTON.

We much regret our inability to give anything like a full and extended history of the life of this man. During the ravages incident to the late war, all his papers, books and other valuable documents were destroyed, and since his death it has been impossible to obtain the information he alone could impart; and information, too, that would be of much interest to his friends and admirers.

He was by nature the most retired man of his intelligence and information in all our country. He was naturally taciturn; a man of few words, especially when in company with strangers.

Alfred S. Fulton was born in the town of Fayetteville, Lincoln county, Tennessee, on the 9th day of September, 1824. He was a son of Col. James Fulton, who was a noted and able lawyer of that place, and who, during his day, was known to and recognized by the profession in Tennessee as one of its ablest and purest members. Nothing is known to us of Col. A. S. Fulton's early boyhood, and we presume there is nothing in it that distinguished him from others of his age and locality. Reaching his "teens," he was sent off to the then celebrated Bingham school, near Hillsboro, North Carolina. Here he remained for some time, and, by his studious application, became thoroughly acquainted with the classics as taught in those days. He returned home, when quite a young man, with a most excellent education, and well-fitted and equipped for the contests and duties of life and manhood.

After his return from school in North Carolina, he spent much of his time in gathering information from the best books he could get hold of, and at times enjoyed his hours of recreation, as was the custom of young men of his day in this country. But it was not long after his return from school until he entered the office of Dr. John V. McKinney, and under his instructions devoted himself to the study and the science of medicine. After spending several months in the office of Dr. McKinney, he attended the medical school at Cincinnati, Ohio. Here he remained for some time, devoting himself and all his energies and time to the mastery of his chosen profession. By those who knew him and were competent to judge of such matters, he was pronounced to be one of the most complete and thoroughly educated medical men in the country. With a mind well filled with the medical sciences and to many of us "mythical mysteries," he began in Fayetteville the practice of medicine.

He soon rose to prominence and took a place in the front rank of the profession. But just here, in the beginning almost of his young and vigorous manhood, and just at the dawning of his success and usefulness as a physician, destined for much good to the community in which he lived, war was declared with Mexico by the government of the United States and volunteers were called for. In obedience to the call, a company was soon raised at Fayetteville, and Dr. Fulton became a member of it. At its organization Pryor Buchanan was elected captain, Dr. Fulton first lieutenant, and Coleman McDaniel second lieutenant. This company was attached to the regiment of Tennessee volunteers commanded by Col. Wm. B. Campbell, afterwards Governor of Tennessee. Abandoning a comfortable home, blessed and surrounded by all things necessary to make him happy, prosperous and successful, leaving kind friends and devoted relatives, laying aside a lucrative practice in its noontide, Dr. Fulton set out for the battle-fields and burning sands of old Mexico.

The terrible hardships and trials and deprivations of that campaign are matters of history, and it is sufficient for us to say he was there and passed through all those scenes of danger and blood. In this war the bravery of the man, the heroism of the young man, came prominently to the front.

The company of which he was a member left Fayetteville on Sunday morning, the 31st of March, 1846, and after encountering many dangers and overcoming many difficulties he landed in Mexico. He was in the battle of Monterey, and there many of his company were killed and wounded. Here it was, in the very hottest of the conflict, that the gallant Captain Allen fell. Lieut. Fulton, while the battle yet raged with fierceness and amid shell and ball, was assigned to the command of Allen's company, and he stood at its head as commander until the battle closed and victory crowned their banner. He was engaged in several skirmishes and did much duty under the burning sun of that country.

Now comes a sad chapter in his life; not one of crime or dishonesty, not one chaparoned by cowardice or poltroonry, but one of exhaustion, languor and disease. The painful toils and hardships of the man during the Mexican campaign will now never be fully and truthfully told. From some cause, his constitution, though of iron build, while out in the wild and malarial atmosphere of that climate, gave way. His health failing so rapidly and to such an alarming extent, he was discharged, as we are informed, and after the close of the war returned home. It should, however, be here stated that before he left the active service and up to the time he was finally stricken down, he remained in command of Capt. Allen's company, whose deeds of heroism have made that company famous, and now fill a bright and glorious page in the history of Tennessee's fame and chivalry.

In this war, Dr. Fulton soon distinguished himself for his gallantry, and won for himself a name and a fame that will cluster around him when stone and marble shall cease to mark in silence his last and final resting place. On these battle-fields he contributed his full share of that devotion and manly courage that gave to Tennessee the proud distinction of "Volunteer State." At all times as quiet and modest as a woman, he was slow to recite his own trials, or to refer in any manner to his acts of kindness and bravery; and after his return home from the Mexican war, it is said by his friends, he was more reticent in manner and habits of life than ever before.

After his return he began to repair and rebuild his constitution and general health, and quietly resuming his profession he soon formed again many warm attachments for his old friends and acquaintances at home, and with very intimate friends he would at times talk freely.

During the late war all his papers and books were lost or destroyed, and much of his life that would be of interest to his friends is lost and can never be supplied.

He was of a peculiar temperament. Passionately devoted to his intimate friends, yet he would at times repel a discourtesy with unmistakable evidences. He entertained a high and exhalted estimate of the duty of man to man, and his whole life was one of strict integrity and truth. He has often said to us that if there was one thing he despised in mankind more than all others it was the "lie" part of his nature and disposition. He seemed to entertain a perfect horror for any individual he ever suspected of falsehood.

Again at home, and with health and strength regained in a great measure, it seemed he was just ripe for the coming event. The great gold excitement burst out in this country like a water-cloud, and emptying its contents swept everything and everybody before it like an avalanche or tornado. The allurements of the gold-fields of California so filled him with their infatuation he soon left home and friends again, and in company with Col. Robt. Farquharson and others began the journey to the Ophir banks of America—the fabulous golden shores and rivers of California.

Here again he was subjected to the most trying hardships and deprivations. After many days and weeks and months spent in hard and fruitless toil and labor, and after many days of suffering, pain and disappointment, he returned home to his "father's house," much depressed by broken health. He began immediately to give his time and attention to his profession, and soon succeeded in getting a good practice.

With his profession he moved smoothly along for several years, giving much time and attention to general reading and gathering up and storing away much valuable information.

Notwithstanding all his modesty and secluded habits of life, but few more intelligent men could be found in one county than he, and when once drawn out in conversation, he was often found to possess a wonderful amount of information on various subjects.

At the time of the beginning of the late war he was again quietly following his chosen profession, but at the sound of the tocsin of war and danger, he entered the ranks of the army and was immediately elected Colonel of the Eighth Regiment of Tennessee Volunteer Infantry, at the organization of that regiment at Camp Trousdale, in Tennessee. With his regiment he soon became a great favorite. His quiet manner of living, his kind and gentle treatment of his men, were so much in contrast with the usual custom of that day and time, that the life of the man at once challenged their admiration and respect. He linked his fortune and his destiny with his regiment; he went where they went, and as they toiled and suffered, he toiled and suffered too. When making long, arduous and terrible marches, though of weak and frail constitution himself, he would often get down off his horse and put some worn-out and exhausted soldier upon his saddle, and march in the ranks himself. When hunger pinched his men, if his headquarters were supplied with rations the men did not have, he would stand and divide with them his last crumb. There was no official bigotry about him. His tent and his camp fire were always filled and surrounded with devoted friends and soldiers. He never sought promotion away from his regiment. He loved his men, and in return his men and soldiers loved him. We knew him well while in the army, and a more noble and benevolent man never lived than Col. Alfred S. Fulton.

Again his health failing him, he was forced to resign and leave us at Corinth, Mississippi. This, indeed, was a dark day for the Eighth Tennessee Regiment. He had passed "through many dangers, toils and snares" with his regiment, and the parting was one of sadness to all.

Returning home after the war closed, he engaged in farming several years, being still feeble and in delicate health. In this occupation he continued until the 5th of February, 1877, when Chancellor Burton appointed him to the responsible position of Clerk and Master of the Chancery Court at Fayetteville, Tennessee. In assuming this office he entered upon important and responsible duties. With perfect accuracy and perfect integrity, he fulfilled and discharged every duty and obligation of the position. In all the varied and complicated duties of the office, not a single one went wrong. He was faithful to the trust and kind to all. Gradually failing in health, he was forced to resign at the October term of the Chancery Court, in 1879.

The end for him was now in sight, and on the 2d day of November following he died, after a short confinement. Thus passed away one of the noblest of men, and Lincoln county may justly feel proud of him as one of her sons.

At his funeral and burial many members of his regiment

came from the adjacent hills and valleys to pay their last sad tribute to his remains. Citizens, doctors, lawyers, merchants, all attended his burial, attesting their appreciation of the man.

After the burial was over, all repaired to the Courthouse, and in common held a "public meeting," at which many touching and beautiful eulogies were pronounced of him and about him, and resolutions were adopted in commemoration of his character, which are parts of the records of our county, and will there remain, we trust, for all time to come.

Thus was consigned to the earth the noble-hearted, lamented Alfred S. Fulton, Colonel of the Eighth Tennessee Regiment.

PART IV.

BRIEF BIOGRAPHICAL SKETCH
—OF—
JOHN H. SAVAGE,

COLONEL SIXTEENTH TENNESSEE REGIMENT.

COL. JOHN H. SAVAGE.

At this time in Middle Tennessee, if not in the entire State, there is no man more generally known than Col. John H. Savage. His career in public or political life thus far has been remarkable, and we, familiar with it, find much food for serious thought. No man brings in question his abilities; and his unblemished and spotless honor stands out grandly and boldly, and to his eternal credit. No man in Middle Tennessee is better characterized for original and independent thought and expression than he; and such men never fail to evoke criticism, and often unjustly.

Col. Savage was born in McMinnville, Warren county, Tennessee, and is now about sixty years old. His father, George Savage, was a soldier in the war of 1812. He was raised on his father's farm, near McMinnville, and there he received all the schooling he ever had, which was indeed limited. His success and prominence are the results, in the main, of his assiduous application to his profession and constant general reading. He is a self made man. During his early boyhood not much is known of him, but we can see running through his speeches and public writings, an unwavering devotion to those he believed to be oppressed or denied their rights and liberties. We find him early in life full of military gallantry, and eager to engage in the sanguinary events of those days.

When the call was made for troops to go and defend Texas in her struggle for independence, he was among the first to volunteer in a company raised in Warren county by Gen. John B. Rogers. Soon after this a call was made by President Jackson for volunteers to go to Florida and defend that country from the murderous work of the Seminoles. A company was raised in his county, and he enrolled himself as one of its members, but this company, from some cause, was not received. Being informed that the company was rejected, Col. Savage, in company with three or four other young men, went to Fayetteville, Tennessee, and on the 4th of July, 1836, joined the brigade of Gen. P. M. Armstrong. He was soon made a member of Capt. Wm. Lauderdale's company of spies; and making that campaign, the many thrilling incidents of which are unnecessary for us to recount here, he was discharged in the city of New Orleans, in January, 1837. He then returned home, and after some time spent in study and preparation, located at Smithville, DeKalb county, and began the practice of law Nov. 12, 1839. He soon attained eminence in his profession, and became a general favorite with the people. So rapid and marked was his career, that the Legislature of 1841 elected him Attorney-General for his district. The duties of his office were so faithfully and satisfactorily discharged, he was chosen elector on the Polk ticket for his district, and in the canvass which he made with the Whig champion of that district, at that time, the Hon. Thomas L. Bransford, he firmly established himself as an orator, and a man of ability, and was soon hailed as the leader of the mountain Democracy of Tennessee.

In 1846, and after war had been declared against Mexico, true to his military impulses and nature, he raised a company of volunteers and again tendered his services to his country, but this company was not accepted.

In 1847, yielding to the earnest solicitations of his friends, and the Democracy of his district, he became a candidate for Congress. After a few days spent in the canvass, and without solicitation on his part, President Polk appointed him major of the Fourteenth regular infantry, then commanded by Col. Wm. Trousdale. Here he entered into active service and was soon on the battle-fields of Mexico. At Vera Cruz he met and formed the acquaintance of President Pierce, and was afterwards a warm supporter of that gentleman for the Presidency.

He was in nearly every battle fought in Mexico—Contreras, Cherubusco and Molino del Rey. At the last-mentioned place, he was severely wounded in the right leg by a shell from the castle of Chepultepec. In this battle Col. Graham, commanding the Eleventh U. S. infantry, was killed, and Major Savage was immediately promoted to the command of the same, and remained as commander of this regiment until the war closed.

Upon his return home to Tennessee, Col. Savage engaged in the canvass and made several speeches for Gen. Cass, who was then the Democratic nominee for President.

At the close of that canvass, he settled down to the practice of his profession at Smithville. In 1849, he was elected to the Congress of the United States over two opponents, Turney and Rogers, by a large majority. In

1851 he was again elected, as he was in 1855 and 1857—making eight years spent in Congress. After the expiration of this last term, being defeated in the next race, he quietly resumed the practice of law, and stood at the head of the bar in his circuit, and accumulated, as we are informed, some property.

During his congressional career he gave many evidences of his ability and statesmanship. His speeches in Congress, many of them, stand to-day as models of oratory; the beautiful language, the glowing eloquence, the lofty flights and passionate, touching appeals, have made the man a great reputation, and one that will pass down to coming generations and be regarded with admiration. Time will take the waspy sting out of the sarcasm and criticism too often hurled at the man, by little hypcritical dwarfs who, like squirming maggots, feed, feast and fatten on the rotten refuse of those whose real worth and nobleness of nature are so far above their own as to be beyond their appreciation or comprehension.

Many extracts of his speeches appear in the best literary works of the land, and are recited and declaimed in almost every school.

As an evidence of the appreciation of many of his speeches, we extract the following from Fields' Scrap-Book, placed alongside the speeches of Clay, Calhoun and Webster:

Discussing, in 1850, in the Congress of the United States, the question of disunion, he said—

"I trust I am not more fearful than other men. If danger comes I expect to be as ready to meet it as I am now anxious to avoid it. I pray to God that I may never again witness the wild work of human destruction, called glorious war. I hope eternal peace may bless the world. With me

> The drying up of a single tear hath more
> Of honest fame than shedding seas of gore.
>
> *   *   *   *   *

But I want no such issue. I love the people of the North. I have always felt that I would peril all that is dear to my native State to protect from lawless violence Massachusetts' humblest citizen or most barren rock. Those of them who know me know that I do. I have never imagined, nor can I imagine, how I could live out of the Union. I have ever hoped that our ship of State, self-poised upon the billows, would gather the tempest in her sails and fly with lightning speed to the home of transcendent national glory, amid the plaudits of an admiring world. And for this I shall still be ready to make any sacrifice except my honor and my right to be free and equal on every foot of land beneath the 'stars and stripes.'"

The bold sentiments here announced at once put after him every fire eater in the country, and for those utterances he paid dearly in the future. Even up to the war many of the so-called leaders made war upon, and did not look upon him as a sound *Simon-pure* secessionist of the Davis and Harris school. It is said that Harris, while Governor of Tennessee, and during the entire war, made constant, yet secret, war upon him, and after the battle of Murfreesboro, or Stone's River, where Col. Savage so distinguished himself, opposed, in some method, his promotion, and a junior Colonel was promoted over Col. Savage, which finally led to his resignation. We do not know the facts or truth of this charge, but we do know that impartial time and an intelligent posterity will not hesitate to award due justice to whomsoever it rightfully belongs.

While in Congress, Col. Savage made another speech, and in reply to the constant assaults on the South and on southern institutions by the fanatics of the North, he said: "But it is not worth while to reason upon this subject while the southern heart is as it is. For the negroes as slaves, we can feel for them. If they were absent we, perhaps, might not lament, but sooner than have them turned loose among us to be our equals, to disgust us by their vices, insult us by their insolence, to degrade our name and posterity by a vile commingling of races, we would pray to God that the ocean wave might blot us from the world, gladly accept the glories of the past, and hope for us no future might be written. I am ready for war, subjugation or extinction; yea, for all the evils that have ever befallen man, rather than this; and if I believed the people of my State, either now or in time to come, would basely submit to be thus degraded, I would this hour leave her and seek a people more noble. But she will not. She cannot."

His speech in Congress on the 17th of December, 1858, on the Old Soldiers' Pension Bill, is one of the ablest and finest of his efforts, but we have not the space to extract from it.

Looking over his career in Congress at this distance, we find it without a blemish. On the good name and fair fame of Tennessee his record sheds additional lustre in the eyes of non-partisan leaders and those not warped by local and personal prejudices. All men will long lament that the fanaticism of the North and the fanaticism of the South buried in their wild rush and turmoil many good and able men in both sections, and filled their places, in many instances, with second-rate, corrupt, ambitious demagogues. In the honesty and fidelity of the people the country is indebted for the stability and grandness of the government, and not to the teaching of many of the "latter day political saints" of the land.

And the man who now aspires to public life, who does not enter into the spirit and shame of stooping down beneath the standard of right and equal justice, has but a poor chance of success in this country. The dawn of a new era may inspire and elevate drooping confidence and hope, and eventually reform and rectify the wrongs of the past and present, and higher standards be erected, but we confess we await its coming with fear and trembling.

When war was a matter of fact between the North and the South, Col. Savage refused to take an active part in organizing companies and regiments. He was reluctant to engage in it, knowing from his experience that it would be one of the most terrible wars ever engaged in by any people. A war veteran, all eyes were turned toward him. His friends, his neighbors and relatives flocked around him. He asked for no command; he sought no high-stilted rank in the army, and would not at that time have accepted any, if tendered him. Yielding to the ties of humanity, and governed by the dictates of a devoted loyalty to his State and his people, he agreed to go with and command the sons of his neighbors and friends.

At Camp Trousdale, at the organization of the Tennessee troops, he was chosen Colonel of the Sixteenth Tennessee infantry regiment, without a single dissenting voice, and true to his promise, he remained with this regiment until unfortunate dissensions which arose among *stilted* officers—not among the men who did the fighting and endured the hardships of the life of a soldier—led to his resignation, at Shelbyville, Tenn.

On the war issues he was emphatically a conservative man, and was not overshadowed by the common fanaticism that swept over this country at that time. When war came, and disease and death and all manner of suffering in its train, he insisted that every man should do his part and perform his full duty.

We are informed that when the Confederate Congress passed the law exempting from military duty all men who owned twenty negroes and upward, he would sometimes make the atmosphere around him a little blue—not that it affected Tennesseans or Tennessee troops to any great extent, but it opened a large loophole for the very class of men in Mississippi and other cotton States to pass out through, who had been most constant and unceasing in their demands for war. It is not our purpose or within our scope to pass any criticisms upon measures or men, but in this one fatal blunder of the South, the death-knell of the Confederacy was sounded. Many people—soldiers, if you choose—soon began to conclude that the whole affair on the part of the South was a rich man's war, but a poor man's fight. All Tennessee troops will bear witness to the existence of this feeling at one time in the army, and we refer to it as a fact connected with our history.

As commander of the Sixteenth regiment during the late war, Col. Savage acquitted himself with the same high honor and daring chivalry he had shown in the Mexican war and in the Florida campaign. Both in the council chamber of the nation and on almost every battle-field of the country, conspicuous in every war the country has engaged in since his boyhood, he has acquitted himself with marked distinction, and without a single blot or stain. Whatever else may be said of him, that he has lived a life distinguished for honesty and true bravery and gallantry no one can question.

It is but a fitting compliment due the man and the soldiers of his regiment that he should be heard to speak for himself at the time he resigned. On the 6th of March, 1863, the following address was read to his regiment, and it needs no comment:

Soldiers of the Sixteenth Regiment, Friends and Companions in Arms:

Nothing but a sense of duty could have forced me to the step which I have taken. When the government selected a junior to command me, it thereby decided that I had not done well in the command of my regiment. Not tired of the war or less devoted to the cause, but it is improper that I should continue in a service where equality is denied me. It is true, I did not ask the government for promotion, and it is also true I did not ask for the command it gave me. In the occurrence which forces me to retire may be seen the hand of a distinguished politician, who stands almost as high in public favor as Andrew Johnson once did, and whose evil offices toward me are as old as my races with Pickett and Stokes.

If selfishness or ambition had controlled my conduct, I should at the beginning of the war have asked to be made a general; but believing that one good regiment was worth many brigades, and with devotion to the cause and with gratitude to my old friends, this induced me to take their children under my charge to protect their lives and honor and teach them to be soldiers. As a regiment I am proud of you, your friends at home are proud of you, and your

State has cause to be. If not the first, your deeds on the field proclaim you the equal of the best regiment in the service. In Virginia and South Carolina you were never off duty, and none dare say any have done better. In the skirmishes around Corinth you proved yourselves better soldiers and marksmen than the enemy, and when the retreat commenced you remained three days upon the Tuscumbia, within six miles of Corinth, confronted by the enemy, and became the rear of the column, an honor that has passed you in silence, while it has been claimed in publications for several commands, brigadiers and colonels.

On the bloody fields of Perryville, far in advance of others, you began the attack on the part of Cheatham's division, which, followed up by the resistless courage of your brothers of Stewart's and Maney's brigades, forever dispelled the cloud of slander and detraction that had darkened the fair fame of the soldiery of our State. The good people south of you never doubted the courage of Tennesseans, and henceforth cowards and miscreants will not dare assail them. At Murfreesboro you were the extreme right of our line of attack, and engaged the enemy's line of battle near its center, while your brigade was marched to the left. Thus isolated and without protection, at a cost of more than half of your numbers, you held in check for three hours the enemy's left wing, and it is believed but for misfortunes not your own you would have maintained the ground till the last. I mingle my tears with yours for the heroic dead, our brothers in arms who sleep upon the fields of Perryville, Murfreesboro and other fields. We can never forget them, and they deserve to be remembered by the country.

If, in my absence, slander should assail me, let not one of you believe that I can cease to care for your welfare or the rights of the Southern people. Character is worth more than money. Continue, my comrades, in the pathway of honor and duty, and if hereafter you shall meet the foe emulate the deeds of former days, that your friends at home may still be proud of you.

My resignation having been accepted, I relinquish the command to the senior officer present, and bid you farewell, hoping that the Great Spirit may guide and protect you through the perils of the future.

JOHN H. SAVAGE,
Colonel Sixteenth Regiment.

SHELBYVILLE, TENN.

The promotion of a junior to the command of the brigade of which the Sixteenth was a part, and other matters, not necessary to further mention, led to this resignation. Here dropped out of the service one of the foremost men in the army; and whatever may have led to this unhappy event, it in nowise lessened the high esteem his men held him in, or those who knew the man. After the close of the war, he returned to the practice of his profession at McMinnville, Tennessee, and had retired from public life, with a determination in his own mind never again to enter any public field as an aspirant. Soon, however, calls were made for him to become a candidate for Congress, and for the Senate and House of Representatives of the General Assembly of Tennessee.

Finally yielding, he was, without opposition, sent to the State Senate, from his district, and there served perhaps for two sessions. He was also sent as a Representative from Warren county for one or two terms, and in each House served his constituents faithfully and well, and with their approval. Over the local question then disturbing the minds of the people of the State, he took a decided and bold stand, and while many thought his position of doubtful propriety, or not in perfect accord with the former teachings of the Democracy of the State, many thought him right. The truth is, he is the father, the life and the light of what was once known in Tennessee as the "low tax" party. Indeed did he sow, while others reaped. He was an aspirant before the Legislature in 1881, for the United States Senate, but was finally defeated, after many ballots, and at one time wanting only a few votes of an election.

His greatest defeat was perhaps in the convention of 1878, at Nashville. He was a candidate for Governor, and had a fair chance for the nomination, but the contest became so bitter and personal, his defeat was almost evident, and he gracefully withdrew in order to secure harmony and the selection of a good man.

Back again among the people, he soon became the advocate of a railroad commission law, a measure intended to protect the people against the unjust and oppressive system of extortion and discrimination practiced on them by railroad companies in Tennessee. This led to much discussion, to a great variety of opinions and much debate among Democrats. Many thought the measure illegal, unjust and unwise, and its application a slow method of confiscation. The measure was modeled into a law by the General Assembly of Tennessee on March the 29th, 1883. By its terms and provisions, three commissioners were to be appointed by the Governor, who were to proceed to enforce it as a law of the State. Gov. Bate made these appointments, conferring on Col. Savage the chairmanship. He qualified under the law on the 25th day of April, 1883, and the commissioners entered into the discharge of their duties. Finally, a bill was filed by some of the railroad companies in the Federal Court at Nashville, attacking the act for its unconstitutionality, and with the question pending in the United States Supreme Court, the subsequent Legislature repealed the law. This was not done, however, till the people at the November election, 1884, had spoken out against it, and by a curious and singular combination of votes, elected a Republican commission upon their public assurances and pledges not to qualify or receive compensation under the act, if elected.

This question and the State debt settlement, and the consequent division in the Democratic ranks, caused many to fall on the political battle field in Tennessee,

> "Whose bones, unburied on the shore,
> Devouring dogs and hungry vultures tore."

In Tennessee it may be safely said that Col. Savage was the champion of the "low-tax" party and the railroad commission measure. With the first issue he insisted, and with much force, power and plausibility, that the State of Tennessee was not legally bound for the payment of State bonds issued to build and equip railroads in Tennessee; that the State, as a State or corporate body, had received no benefit for her acts of accommodation to the companies, but that the companies had all the profit and all the property, and ought to pay the bonds issued for them and to them.

Without stopping to call into question the wisdom of these measures, we are constrained to award to him a pure, honest conviction, and no one to-day has ever uttered or insinuated one word of dishonor against the man. We have been no admirer of the position taken by him on these questions. Indeed, we have differed with him on

State issues all along the line, but we shall do him justice if we know it, and declare that no man in Tennessee politics has been more foully abused and slandered, and no man, in our opinion, will go down to the grave with a purer character or purpose than Savage, "the Old Man of the Mountains." He still lives in a good, old, ripe age, and no man in Tennessee can feel a more conscious pride than he of his fidelity to every trust, though partisan clamor and partisan meanness have howled long and loud at his heels. There are men in Tennessee to-day, filling high offices, who are vastly his inferiors, both as to ability and honesty.

But in conclusion of this brief and imperfect sketch of a life remarkable in many particulars, a life spent and made up on fields of battle and blood and on the hustings and in the legislative halls of the country, both State and National, we beg to close with an extract from one of his beautiful speeches, delivered in the House of Representatives of the Tennessee Legislature, while a bill was pending before it to deny the benefit of the exemption laws of the State to poor persons moving out of it. It illustrates the grandness of the man, the tenderness of his nature, and his undying devotion to the poor and oppressed of earth. These sublime sentiments here uttered, should exalt the man in the hearts and affections of all good people. Let spiteful little officials, who have crawled into office and into power through back windows and back doors, criticise and howl at him till they die of their own shame:

Mr. Speaker: I have great respect for the gentlemen of the Judiciary Committee and for the members of this House, but every impulse of my nature rebels against the spirit and policy of this bill. In my opinion, it is neither wise, nor humane, nor merciful. The people of these States should be of one blood, one bone, one flesh, and one destiny. Nor am I unmindful of the still broader doctrines taught from on high, that the human race is, or ought to be, a universal brotherhood, in which the poor man or woman, to the remotest bounds of the earth, is our neighbor and our friend.

Not only is this bill wrong in principle, but it requires but little experience or imagination to see that innumerable wrongs and injuries will be imposed upon the unfortunate poor, from which the humanity and mercy of its advocates would shrink back in shame. It is almost certain that men as noble as any on your soil have, in other days, to better their condition, gone to other States and now, reduced to abject poverty and want, like the prodigal son, would gladly return to friends and kindred and the home of their youth. It may be it is your sister or your beautiful daughter, or the daughter of your neighbor, who has been permitted in the bloom of her youth to accompany the man of her choice beyond your borders, has been stricken in her family by sickness, misfortune and death, who is now a poor widow with infant children, without friends, in a strange land, pale, emaciated, broken down in health as well as pecuniarily. Nature and necessity would present to her unhappy mind the babbling brooks, beautiful flowers and trusted friends of her former home. She resolves to return to father and mother and kindred friends in Tennessee. Perhaps she has nothing left from the wreck of her husband's fortune but a half starved horse, mule or yoke of cattle, a broken down cart, wearing apparel, household and kitchen furniture. It is death to stay. Hope points her onward and the journey is begun, but unfortunately she is in a State that has followed the example the Judiciary Committee would have us set. Perhaps, on the first or at a later day, before she reaches the State line, at the instance of some merciless and persistent creditor, an officer overtakes her and seizes every article of property, including the scanty allowance of meat and bread for the journey, leaving the poor woman and her children to perish or live on charity. It is more important that men, women and children shall live happy, than that the Shylock shall have his pound of flesh.

My understanding of the duties of statesmanship forbids my support of a policy that will often be used as a means to oppress or destroy the poor, and but seldom to defeat the dishonest debtor. Sir, my nature and my statesmanship must change before I can support the bill.

www.ingramcontent.com/pod-product-compliance
Lightning Source LLC
Chambersburg PA
CBHW020111170426
43199CB00009B/486